Contents

BIRMINGHAM & ~~~~ ~~~
CO~~~~ ~~~ OF N~~ ~~~ ~~~~~~~

D~TE: 5 - 95

ACC. NO: 00023375

CLASS: 371.9209411

SITE: QE

KU-567-525

BI 0870907 6

Meeting Special Education
A Scottish Perspective

Series Editors

Gwynedd Lloyd *and* Judith Watson

This item may be recalled before the date stamped below.
You must return it when it is recalled or you will be fined.

NORMAL LOAN

25 NOV 1996	22 NOV 2006	
29 MAY 1997	20 APR 2007	
05 JAN 1998		
24 APR 1999		
26 APR 2001		
10 MAY 2006		24hr Renewals 0121 331 5278 or online at http://library.uce.ac.uk
20 JUL 2006		

Moray House Publications
Holyrood Road, Edinburgh
EH8 8AQ

UNIVERSITY OF
INFORMATION SERVICES
CENTRAL ENGLAND

60984 81800

Other titles in this series

Chosen with Care? Responses to Disturbing and Disruptive Behaviour
Volume 2
Edited by Gwynedd Lloyd

Special Educational Needs Beyond 16
Volume 3
Edited by Alison Closs

A Curriculum For All? 5-14 and Special Educational Needs
Volume 4
Edited by Elizabeth Jordan
Due Winter 1994

Working with Communication Difficulties
Volume 5
Edited by Judith Watson

All titles, plus publications catalogue, available from:
Moray House Publications, Holyrood Campus,
Holyrood Road, Edinburgh EH8 8AQ
Tel: 0131-558 6398   Fax: 0131-558 3428

All rights reserved. No part of this publication may be reproduced, stored in a retrieval system, or transmitted in any form or by any means, electronic, mechanical, photocopying, recording or otherwise, without prior permission of Moray House Publications.

First published 1991
Reprinted 1994
© Judith Watson

Printed and bound by Bell and Bain Ltd, Glasgow

UNIVERSITY OF
CENTRAL ENGLAND

Book no. 08709076

Subject no.371.920941

INFORMATION SERVICES

Foreword

G P D Gordon
HM Chief Inspector of Schools

I am very pleased to have the privilege of writing the foreword to a new publication on Special Educational Needs. Gwynedd Lloyd and Judith Watson are to be congratulated for taking on such a demanding but commendable initiative.

There is no doubt that there has been a lot going on in special educational needs in recent years. The reports by the Warnock Committee and HM Inspectorate pioneered new perceptions in the 1970s, and developments in the 1980s, emanating principally from the 1981 legislation, led to a more complex and informed debate on the identification and assessment of pupils' needs and the means of fulfilling them. The trend towards recording the needs of more children, the discussion on forms of integration, the increasing use of new technologies, and a growing appreciation that there is a continuum of need, with no neat dividing lines, have led all of us with an interest and concern for children to look more carefully at the range and quality of the curriculum which must be offered, the ways in which we effectively use the expertise and experience of parents and professionals and the availability and deployment of material resources.

The first edition of *Meeting Special Educational Needs: A Scottish Perspective* reflects the challenge which we face in addressing these issues in the early 1990s. The opportunity to read and think about them in such a publication, and, importantly, subsequently engage in resolving them can only be to the advantage of Scottish children.

Introduction

Judith Watson

In planning this first volume of *Meeting Special Educational Needs: A Scottish Perspective*, I was very aware of the need for a unifying theme, while also wishing to draw on a wide range of contributors. The broad theme is innovation in relation to children and young people with severe learning difficulties: innovation in provision, curricular innovation, or innovatory ideas arising from research.

Several contributors address issues of terminology in describing their work, and Professor Hogg considers it at more length. The different chapters encompass the range of young persons extending from those with the most profound learning difficulties, normally associated with severe sensory and physical impairments, to those with less, but nonetheless serious difficulties in learning. No contribution in this volume is based on work in an ordinary mainstream educational setting.

The authors comprise a range of professionals, including classroom and head teachers, psychologists, academic researchers and speech therapists. Some have become known to the editor through professional college courses, some through publications and conferences, and some through direct contact within professional settings. Lecturers in colleges of education are greatly privileged in being acquainted with a wide range of experienced teachers undertaking courses, and in subsequently maintaining contact with many of them in their continuing professional development. Such continuing links partly account for the East Coast bias in the present volume.

A second unifying feature is that all the work described has been carried out in Scottish schools, colleges or universities with Scottish children or young adults. It will have relevance well beyond the United Kingdom, as the special needs of those with learning difficulties have common elements wherever their geographical location, but the Scottish education system and traditions will also have a distinctive influence. Within the relatively small Scottish population, the Scottish Office Education Department plays a central role. Many educational research projects and curricular developments are initiated and supported by the SOED and their publications are normally well disseminated and publicised. Other work, such as that represented in the present volume, is conducted without such support and tends to be less well-known though innovative and potentially very valuable. Scottish educationists are accused sometimes of accentuating differences with those south of the Border and of turning a wilful blind eye to developments there. This is justifiable criticism at times but the converse also sometimes applies.

The volume is divided into three parts. The first comprises accounts of curriculum development undertaken by practising teachers, and by one speech therapist. All represent initiatives in responding to the immediate perceived needs of pupils and staff in special school settings. They have therefore grown out of professional reflection and awareness. All have already elicited interest in their respective geographical settings and all deserve wider dissemination. All demonstrate the scope hitherto enjoyed by individual members of staff and individual schools for developing their own curricular initiatives, and all demonstrate how impressive such individual efforts may be, though undeniably time, energy and resource-consuming.

In the second section are papers describing research undertaken by psychologists and by a clinical research fellow in speech therapy. Two were direct responses to requests for help, from teachers dealing with pupils whose behaviour was exceptionally challenging, and from a parents' association. All four include theoretical discussions and useful references, and all have in my view direct and relevant practical implications for those whose jobs involve day to day contact. None is in the least detached from every day realities: all show sensitive awareness of wider issues, alongside academic rigour. Such work is an essential and effective bridge over the much-lamented gap between theory and practice in education.

The last group of papers describe innovations in provision. Significantly all began as a result of pressure from parents. The three described are unique in Scotland. The authors discuss events leading to their formation and the principles underlying their planning along with the constraints and difficulties and compromises which will always have to be made in practice. The tripartite layout of this volume should not mask the striking emergence of recurrent concerns in all three sections. A brief discussion of some of these follows. Readers will no doubt identify many more links between different contributions.

Jennifer Wishart's major work with a large number of children who have Down's Syndrome, emphasises how motivational factors may depress their performance increasingly with age to well below optimal level. Her descriptions of children's adoption of avoidance strategies, opting out and ready reliance on adult help, will resonate with many teachers and parents. Her finding that enabling pupils to control their own learning increases motivation and better consolidation, links well with Shona Pinkerton's exciting results. Her pupils learned very quickly to control rewarding sensory feedback through their own normally ineffective movements when these were made potent by technology. Shona Pinkerton reports how only feedback that was contingent on their own actions led to dramatic increases in their levels of activity and involvement. Jennifer Wishart makes the very important point that children with severe learning difficulties are likely to experience a great deal of feedback which is not directly related to their own performance (for example by being only passively involved in tasks, or being rewarded for trying, however inaccurately) and that they will inevitably have difficulty in drawing conclusions about the effects of their actions in such experiences.

A strong emphasis on pupil control and initiative is also made by Christine Knight and by Anne Edmonstone in their papers on communication. Here the aim is to promote interactions, verbal or non-verbal, in which the control and pace of communication is shared as in normal, non-didactic conversations. The emphasis is on facilitating the awareness in even the most developmentally delayed and physically impaired pupils that they can affect their social environment, other people. Pupil activity, staff responsiveness, shared control and mutual enjoyment are ingredients. The skills-based curriculum is criticised for its rather different emphasis and for sometimes inadvertently encouraging passivity and dependency in pupils in its concentration on repetitive tasks, designed to develop particular skills.

Anne Edmonstone's ideas for games emphasise variety, fun, and surprise within an oft-repeated framework or 'script' which has become familiar to the child. Elizabeth Dean and Jane Davidson adopted the idea of scripts and general event representation theory as a basis for designing effective speech therapy for pre-school children with Down's Syndrome. Their encouraging results indicate how children's communication and language may advance when the cognitive demands of a task are lessened because of its familiarity to the child but enough novelty and variety is retained to interest them. The same general principle probably accounts for the effectiveness of Margaret Mackay and Maureen Lorimer's recipe reading programme in their school. The standard recipe format is a script, directly linked to physical actions and a tangible edible end product. The written and spoken language linked with activity, in a very meaningful task, again appears to promote learning. As Andrew Jahoda's interviews showed reading and writing skills are valued by those with learning difficulties in the post-school years and should be promoted as far as possible.

Parents' views and needs are recognised by all authors as crucially important in planning. Indeed, as noted, all the new provisions described here were the direct result of persistent, informed, parent pressure. In the programmes for pre-school children described by Catriona Dairon and by Elizabeth Dean and Jane Davidson regular participation by a parent or other committed adult is integral, as the programmes are designed to be continued and generalised within the home. With older pupils the curricular developments devised by Jo Eales and by Margaret Mackay and Maureen Lorimer both emphasise the importance of school experiences being integrated and consistent with those at home.

Jo Eales describes early joint consultation between staff and parents about the nature and content of a school's 'Growing Up' Health Education programme and how parents' suggestions influenced its design and implementation. Shared knowledge between school and home encourages consistency in approach, enhances understanding of the child in each, and fosters mutual respect.

Respect for the individual underlies the 'gentle teaching' approach which is arousing considerable interest, and its theoretical basis and practical application is discussed by Sally Cheseldine. The emphasis is placed on acceptance of and respect for the individual 'in spite of often repulsive behaviours'. Challenging behaviour has to be seen as a form of meaningful communication. What seems to be emerging as an important issue here is that of the individual's self worth, also emphasised by Andrew Jahoda and by Josephine Eales. The latter describes decision making and a sense of responsibility for one's own actions as being at the core of health education and her chapter illustrates activities which appear to be effective in achieving this in school. Feeling good about oneself, feeling confident enough to say 'no' and feeling one is taken seriously as a person, relate to Andrew Jahoda's research with adults. He suggests that group discussions at school and beyond can be very useful in helping people to develop and maintain feelings of self worth and positive identities.

Sue Harland's paper clearly sets out some of the practical and organisational complexities involved in running a school which is open virtually all year, many of which seem to be almost insurmountable. She expresses concerns about some potentially negative, unplanned effects such as increasing isolation of the child within the family neighbourhood and reducing the likelihood of family holidays for the child. Perhaps the most serious concern is that by its very availability such provision may indicate to some parents that it is better than what they can offer at home. Such an unintended result could also occur with the creation of a purpose built centre closely linked with all the expert services available in a University as described by Philip Seed and James Hogg. A recurring danger in this area is that of 'deskilling' parents by expertise and specialised services.

Philip Seed outlines preparatory research and decision making in which it is clear that potential clients' existing social networks were investigated and a great deal of consideration given to the wide range of possible approaches to an exciting new development. James Hogg, holder of the Chair of Profound Disabilities at the University of Dundee, in the concluding chapter of the third section of the book, asks fundamental questions about what is meant by 'quality of life' and how that of adults with profound disabilities can be enhanced to the greatest possible degree. This discussion neatly brings us back to our starting point, emphasising along with the other contributors to the book, the growing importance of functional and interactive approaches to the curriculum, and concluding that enhanced quality of life must feature personal control, community involvement, affective involvement, choice and self determination.

Active Learning through the use of Microtechnology

Shona Pinkerton

Introduction

> It is not their special needs with which I am primarily concerned, but their normal needs: their need to have an enjoyable and estimable life and to be able to interact satisfyingly with their environment and its people, things and demands. Sometimes we require special techniques and technology to help us meet our needs. Only when they are wanting are we truly handicapped. (Goldenberg 1979).

This statement was referring to children with cerebral palsy, autism or deafness. However, it is considered here to be applicable in a far wider context. Indeed such experiences should be fundamental to everyone, whatever the multiplicity or complexity of their impairments. The following is a description of a study undertaken in 1989, which considers how technology can open up a range of interactional opportunities for pupils with profound learning difficulties with additional sensory and/or physical impairment. It also examines the effect such experiences can have both on the pupils and on the staff working with them. The encouraging results of the initial study have provided a platform for on-going developments which may be mentioned here but will be fully documented during 1992.

The background to the study

The study group comprised a class of six pupils with profound learning difficulties, aged between twelve and nineteen years. They each have severe physical impairment: one girl could sit unaided for a few seconds, another when wearing her surgical jacket could raise her head with considerable effort, while one of the boys could use his right arm and hand to reach out to lightly touch an object. Some of these children had additional auditory and/or visual impairment. For these pupils their earlier experiences of life had been heavily weighted towards their care firstly in a social work provision and later in a combined social work and education situation. Often their needs had been anticipated and much had been done for them, which in effect created a rather passive environment.

When the Education Dept. assumed full responsibility for staffing the school in 1987, the class team developed a curriculum focused on involving the pupils, encouraging their communication and active participation.

> Much of current cognitive psychological theory is dominated by the idea that passive observation of our environment is insufficient for learning. (Goldenberg 1979)

Influenced by such theory, the emphasis was firstly on encouraging social interaction between staff and pupils and between pupils and their peers, which meant responding to the communication signals sent out by the pupils in the form of body language, facial expressions and vocalisations. This implies great responsibilities for the staff, requiring observational skills and receptiveness. In this sense, the staff team felt that the pupils were able to be active participants. The emphasis was also on doing with the children and not simply to or for them. From teeth-cleaning and face-washing to painting or making music, each pupil, in his own way, was supported and encouraged to be actively involved. However, such support was mainly co-active, guiding the pupil through the experience. In some cases, a pupil would require only cooperative assistance, where they required less physical support. On occasion a pupil could participate reactively, or independently, but often it seemed that for considerable effort they received a minimal reward. Undoubtedly valuable though these experiences are, the staff team continued to seek out opportunities to extend the pupils' physical control of their environment.

Piaget considered that learning comes from the subject's own activity. This suggests independence and autonomy for the child and as this was still not readily available to the pupils in a physical sense, this became the focus for further consideration both in theory and in practice within the study early in 1989. It is important to note, however, that while the ensuing study relates to the use of technology, it should not be seen in isolation. Instead, by extending the opportunities for interaction and active participation it is encompassing the philosophy which was being developed in all areas of the curriculum and reflecting the global experience of the child.

A child centred approach

Throughout the study control was importantly to remain with the pupils. This was to allow each individual to structure the experience himself, starting by using his own abilities and allowing freedom to develop in the way which he chose. This did not mean that there were no parameters to an activity or that there were no objectives. Quite the contrary, for considerable adult involvement was required in assessing and setting up the elements of what and how to control, in such a way as to offer the highest opportunities for successful active involvement, from which the individual would create his own experience. Objectives, rather than being predetermined by the adult, emerged as each pupil interacted with his environment.

This contrasts with the behaviourist approach, where the actual experience is adult directed, with set objectives, and a range of physical, verbal and gestural prompting are used to achieve the end product. Often the rewards within a behavioural approach are extrinsic, while it is suggested here that the process of being in control offered in the interactive model is a reward in its own right, being intrinsically motivating. The child centred approach to the use of technology was selected as it was a natural extension of the approach being used with good results in other curricular areas with the group.

This conflicts with the views of Rostron and Sewell (1983) who suggest, 'children will not make sufficient progress if placed in control, particularly children suffering from some form of learning handicap'. While they do not advocate a solely behaviourist model of intervention, they choose to consider either approach when assessing individual needs. However, within this study using an interactive approach there were very interesting results which did allow the monitoring of contingency awareness and learning within the study group.

Resources used to facilitate autonomy

Having access to a powerful technology which one can control oneself and with which one can get direct immediate feedback creates such a striking change in these children's sense of autonomy. (Goldenberg 1979)

The first objective of the study was to try to give each of the pupils total freedom to be in control in spite of their limited and quite individual physical abilities. Therefore, when assessing the technology available, suitable equipment had to be able to be tailored to meet individual needs both in accessing the technology and in the range of stimuli it could control. A variety of options were considered which could take account of very limited independent physical abilities. Also, while the pupil's previous independence, perhaps in touching a squeaky toy, had offered little results for a lot of effort, or rather a small 'effect' for a big 'cause', it was important to be able to turn this round and offer a small 'cause' giving a big 'effect'.

After consideration, for the study, a Mains Switcher and a range of switches and electrically operated stimuli were chosen. The Mains Switcher, designed by the CALL Centre, Dept of Education, Edinburgh University, is a mains powered environmental control unit which is operated by a single switch. It allows versatility in accessing, as generally any switch terminated with a 1/4" jack plug can be used to operate it. It is shortly to be marketed by QED[1].

This small shoebox sized unit can control any mains powered electrical appliance up to 750w and has a variable timed setting of zero to seven seconds.

Using an adaptor, two stimuli could be operated together eg. lights and fan. This would mean that operating a switch, by a single action already within the pupil's repertoire, would activate stimuli for several seconds.

Moving beyond the study, further opportunities can be created using a switch operated timed toy controller[2]. Equally, using a BBC Master and appropriate switches, pupils can control visual and auditory stimuli direct from the computer, or by using a computer interface box with a toy adaptor[2] switching can control adapted toys. Further, by connecting a cassette lead[3] and cassette recorder to the cassette part of the BBC Computer, pupils can control favourite music or story tapes. Within the evaluation, the possibilities for extending the potential of the 'Snoezelen Room' or multi sensory room will also be looked at, to show how it can be accessible for those with limited physical abilities, through using similar environment control technology.

Putting theory into practice

> For children accustomed to a passive role, the new environment must be made especially attractive to encourage learning the new active way. Building self-discipline, self-esteem and independence then become possible. Any activity that varies the environment has potential for stimulating learning and enhancing motivation. Those that provide the experience of control are particularly important. (Goldenberg *et al.* 1984)

What to control?

A range of assessments of each of the pupils were underway by January 1989, and reviewing and reassessing became a continuing and ever present part of the study. One aspect of the assessment was to establish for each pupil a range of stimuli which they would choose or would enjoy being in control of, and this also took account of the intensity and optimum positioning of the stimuli.

An assessment of the functional use of the senses was updated, using the guidelines from 'Identifying the needs of Profoundly Mentally Handicapped Children', (Browning 1983). Also more finely tuned visual assessments were carried out for some of the pupils using a functional visual assessment package (Aitken and Buultjens). This was supplemented by information from a parents' questionnaire where parents had been asked to suggest favourite electrical items which they felt interested their child.

Staff, with the support of the speech therapist, used an observation sheet to note pupils' non-verbal but highly communicative responses to different electrical stimuli and the physiotherapist's guidelines for encouraging good positioning were taken into account. These taken all together helped to establish a range of stimuli to use with each pupil. The actual range varied from brightly flashing disco lights to soft lantern lights, taped stories, popular, classical or jazz music, foot spa, fan, food mixer, hair drier......the list is endless.

How to control?

A surface assessment which examines only physical abilities and disabilities.....is not considered satisfactory. (Millar *et al.*)

This statement helps to place the assessment of functional movement or other means of accessing within a network of variables, not to be divorced from a wide range of intrinsic and extrinsic influences. So in assessing the accessing potential of the pupils, time was taken to take account of fluctuations in mood, motivation, and general wellbeing.

Each of the pupils had a range of positions recommended by the physiotherapist: sitting, prone standing in a flexistand or supine board, side lying, prone over a multiwedge are examples. The class team compiled information through classroom observations of the actual functional movement which a pupil displayed in each of their positions. The observations were specific about the part of the body which was controlled and the actual position which was displayed. A pupil who could raise his head in a prone stander, would likely have a different ability in another situation, and this provided a small range of accessing points dependent on the position of the pupil at any given time.

During this process there was the opportunity to consider the implications of motivation. It became clear that each pupil had a range of movements which could be performed more easily and were therefore used most often. Other movements requiring more effort were mainly used when extremely motivating situations arose. For the purposes of the study, movements within the first group were sought. It should also be noted that the movements did not have to be hand or arm movements. Head turning or lifting, foot or leg action, indeed any controlled movement from any part of the body was acceptable. The main aim was to facilitate environmental control and provided that a switch matched the movement being displayed, it was not the intention to enforce a more demanding movement. However, again moving beyond the study, there were valuable opportunities to incorporate physiotherapy aims to extend the frequency of use of the higher level abilities which the pupils displayed. Having identified a repertoire of actions for each pupil, it was important to establish that they were indeed actions which the physiotherapist would wish to encourage.

In the long term, the expertise of the physiotherapist could guide the class team through the patterns of movement to be encouraged and those to be discouraged. By inhibiting primitive reflex patterns, there would be the opportunity to build a foundation of normal movement patterns and the ongoing opportunity for further physical development. In the short term, this was taken into account when there was a choice of actions to be encouraged by a pupil. If the only action available had been less desirable from a physiotherapist's viewpoint, it would have been used initially to allow the pupil to experience control, in the hope that the motivation of the experience would identify more appropriate means of accessing. The involvement of an occupational therapist is also desirable when considering hand function or other functional movements, and while the school now has this service, it was not in place at the time of the study.

And so to the next stage which was to match a switch to the pupil's action. It was not considered adequate to use a finite group of switches and simply allocate the one closest to the ability of the pupil. Instead importance was placed on matching the physical ability of the pupil and the action required to operate the switch. With the support of the CALL Centre, switches were available on loan to test their suitability. Using a relatively small bank of switches, it was possible to match the abilities of all six pupils in the study. Each of them was able to operate at least one switch, and more often, several switches with different actions; a tilt switch on Jane's head was operated by her raising her head, and Oliver could use a head action to press a switch positioned on his chair at the back of his head. Danny, using his feather-light finger movements could operate an SB Systems touch switch which required no pressure, simply contact with the switch. Similar examples could be cited for each of the group. What use they made of this facility will be expanded in due course. Since the study, the school has invested in a wide range of switches and environmental control units. In the last two years many more switches have become available from a range of suppliers. [1, 2, 3, 4] They take account of much finer movements and may have adjustable settings to suit individual abilities. Examining switches could merit an independent study and space does not allow this, other than to stress that time is well spent investigating the potential of many of those more recently available and matching an appropriate switch to the needs of the child.

> If it is discovered that a child, who is severely or profoundly impaired, does indeed make meaningful use of a computer, then there may be difficulties in generalizing from the learning which occurs in this microworld. This necessitates development of curricular intentions as to how this microworld will be fitted within the macroworld of their environment. (Aitken 1988)

By establishing the opportunity for control, using different switches and actions in different positions, there was the added advantage of providing a more generalized learning experience. Again it is stressed that the use of technology complemented the wider curriculum aims.

A team approach

For pupils who are multiply impaired with profound learning difficulties, the means of facilitating active learning, and encouraging autonomy, becomes the remit of the multidisciplinary team whose expertise covers every aspect of the whole child. (Sigel 1979)

It is already clear that a range of professionals require to be involved when planning and implementing an appropriate curriculum with children who have such complex needs, and the importance of gaining an overall picture of the 'whole child' can not be overemphasised. A true team approach would ideally involve all of the relevant therapists and the room team meeting to discuss various issues. However, staffing resources dictate the practicalities and realities of a situation and during the study it was rarely possible to do so. It highlights the teacher's position as a coordinator of the inputs. Care has to be taken to avoid a fragmented approach to assessment and good practice demands that therapists, teachers and support staff take account of the whole child and the interaction of each of their areas of expertise. Throughout this, there should also importantly be involvement with the family, encouraging their input as valuable members of the team.

Method of observation and data collection

By early March, while the experience was still new to the pupils, formal evaluations took place using time sampling procedures, by extracting pupils individually into the familiar classroom with reduced distractions, while the rest of the class worked outside in the base. A full evaluation was split into four consecutive sections each lasting five minutes with the pupil remaining in one of their recommended positions throughout. Observation sheets were both qualitative and quantitative, allowing recording of the actual activities which were observed and the number of times they occurred.

Observation one: a baseline observation with no intentional stimuli.

Observation two: the mains switcher with the appropriate switch carefully in position, along with the stimuli selected from the earlier observations, but the power supply was **not** connected.

Observation three: the same set-up as in two, but with the power supply connected: opportunity to experience reactive participation.

Observation four: the stimuli remained in position, while the switcher and switch were removed. The stimuli were connected directly to the power supply and operated continuously without any participation.

Several full sets of observations of four of the pupils in different positions were collected over four weeks, with video recordings supplementing the written recordings. Of the other two pupils, one had medical problems, and the other became over anxious during observations one and two, and it was decided to allow her to continue to enjoy the reactive experience outwith the study.

Evaluating the experience

Considering the results both qualitatively and quantitatively, there were many interesting points to note. Firstly, all the pupils could and did use their switch to control the stimuli. The frequency with which they participated varied, but each could be seen to be making considerable efforts, with vocalisations, smiles, laughs and physical effort often increasing by between three and four hundred per cent during reactive participation.

The actions which were required to operate the switch could be seen with low frequency in the baseline observations and these actions increased dramatically when in control of the stimuli. For example, Danny, positioned supine wearing leg splints, operated a mercury tilt switch on his right hand. During the base line observation, he raised his hand five times. During observation three, reactive participation, he operated the switch controlling the stimuli fifteen times, and with a much more vigorous action than had been seen previously. This was in the ratio of 3:1 over the baseline.

Motivating factors - the stimuli or the control?

In each case, the ability to control was visible and motivating as participation increased considerably over baseline levels. Also, when comparing the reactive participation (observation three) with the passive experience (observation four) throughout the many sets of data, there are clear indications of heightened awareness and increased attention span during reactive participation. Effort and determination could be seen as well as increased vocalisation and general movement, and this level of participation often extended far beyond the five minutes sample. In comparison during the passive experience pupils tended to show greatly diminished interest in the stimuli.

It appeared that the motivation was in experiencing control. For example, Kate, during reactive participation, operated the switch seventeen times and was wide-eyed, full of upper body and head movement. During the passive experience, the excitement seemed to have been removed along with the switch. It seemed that the enjoyment was in the task, the successful participation an

During the reactive participation, Kate often looked at
source. She did not sustain this during the passive exper
observations suggest that it was as though they no longer see
As she has both visual and auditory agnosia, it is interesti
responded to these stimuli when she was in control of then

Time and time again, pupils reached out, touched or ʃ
could not give examples of other situations which showed such intense acɯvɪ_
obvious enjoyment. For the blind children within the study, the development of
proprioception can be clearly seen on the video material. Touching and activating
the switch, raising an arm and then lowering it to find the switch again, losing
contact with the switch and finally relocating it by problem solving for themselves
are a few examples of the skills which were displayed.

A multi sensory room accessible to pupils with a physical impairment

A number of schools are beginning to develop multi sensory rooms. For physically
able pupils, there is usually an element of choice, for the pupil can move to the part
of the room which interests them, perhaps to smell the aroma from the smell tube[5],
feel the vibrations from the bubble tube [5], position themselves to experience the
stunning visual effects created by using fibre optics [5], or watch projected images
spinning round a room through the use of a panoramic rotator [5] attached to a
projector. While there is an element of choice, and the pupil may be motivated to
actively explore the stimuli, this does not necessarily extend to offering the pupils
control over these stimuli. A multi sensory room set up in this way would offer even
less versatility for pupils such as those within the study. For them the room may
offer no more than a passive experience and the study suggested that in comparison
to situations over which the pupil had control, the passive experience creates far
less interest, awareness and attention in the pupils.

Therefore, if account is to be taken of the value of control, as in the current
study and further advocated in much of the aforementioned literature, it would
be extremely worthwhile to incorporate similar environmental control units such
as the mains switcher used in the study, or master controllers [5] which offer similar
facilities. This would allow the pupils as in the study to operate a switch within their
range of ability to create the effect which they chose. Moving beyond the study,
further work with more physically able children has shown their delight in
controlling the stimuli using switches appropriate to their abilities. This would
suggest that control within the multi sensory room using a range of switches would
not be restricted in value to those with limited physical abilities but would offer
generally the chance to create the environment rather than simply exploring a
preset environment.

...tingency awareness

...he pupils displayed clear signs of contingency awareness. In section two of each observation, pupils tended to begin by making the necessary movement to activate the switch. As the power was not connected, the expected effect was not achieved. After several tries, in general, their attempts ceased or became half hearted and occasional. This highlights the need for careful assessment of accessing abilities, in order to facilitate successful participation. Success in observation three could be seen to foster self esteem, and was intrinsically motivating while the failure to gain control in observation two brought initially frustration and finally withdrawal from further attempts.

Timing

It became clear that not only was it important that the pupil had control of the activity, but also that this in turn gave control of the pace. It was possible to identify when and how often individuals operated their switch during the five minutes of reactive participation. Many of the pupils started slowly during the first minute, and gradually built up to an intense level of participation around the third minute, before slowing down again. One interesting variation on this was frequently shown by Mary, who often took two minutes or more to begin switching, but once underway she continued to build up the frequency over the following minutes. It is all too easy for staff to build in timing which suits their own makeup, and this can be quite out of step with the pupil. Following our observations with Mary, we began to look more carefully at her responses in other situations. We went on to discover that similarly, she generally required some considerable time to build up to give, for example, a facial response to a taste. This had implications for the manner in which we had been offering drinks choices and we were able to use the information to adjust the timing in this and other situations to take account of Mary's pace.

Staff observations and expectations

Throughout the study, staff were encouraged to use their observation skills to note the pupils' responses in a variety of situations, from the assessment stage through to the evaluation. While we all considered that we took account of the pupils' non-verbal communications prior to the study, we equally had to agree that we had become more receptive and responsive to finer details. Our awareness was heightened during the four months of the study and beyond as we continue to extend the response-governed opportunities offered to the pupils. Further, as we see the abilities of the pupils unmasked through the use of technology, it has developed our expectations of each pupil in a wider sense. Pupils have been able to demonstrate cognitive skills, develop their attention and problem solving abilities, and generally operate at a level higher than had previously been expected.

A very interesting example can be cited in the case of Danny. Beyond the study he has gone on to use two mains switchers set up with switches, each of which he can control. They have been set up to control tape recorders with different types of music, and Danny has been recorded interacting with each in turn over a few minutes, until he has made a choice and then he has continued operating solely the chosen switch/music. After several minutes enjoying the music, the tape recorders were plugged into the opposite switchers. Danny continued to use the switch which had been playing his chosen music for only a few times before turning his attention to the other switch. On retracing his preferred music, he smiled and vocalised happily and began to concentrate his efforts using this switch to achieve his desired music. This can highlight the undiscovered potential of some of our pupils. It also gives staff as well as pupils great encouragement. The use of such technology has proved a valuable facilitator, for when physical limitations are preventing someone from displaying their abilities and their communication is non-verbal and open to interpretation, one can only guess at the possibilities which lie untested or underdeveloped. Such exciting findings have given the impetus for further research.

Conclusion

For these pupils interacting with the environment and being in control is seen as an important feature of their learning experience. The study has shown the value of facilitating without directing such experiences, and that this can be made available taking account of individual's limited physical abilities and early stage of development. While the group may often require a high level of care, sometimes called 'special care', this should not be mistaken for total care, which suggests a withdrawal of all pupil control.

The study has shown clearly that for the young people in the study there is enormous value in experiencing stimulating and motivating self directing opportunities. It can unmask their abilities, and provide opportunities to develop them further, increasing their enjoyment, self esteem, attention, cognition, effort and activity. Technology has shown that it has the potential to bring such valuable experiences to fruition and that it is indeed a useful resource with which to extend the possibilities for active participation through interactive learning.

References

Aitken, S (1988). Computer-Aided instruction with the multiply impaired. *Journal of Mental Deficiency Research,* 32.

Browning, M *et al.* (1983). *Identifying the needs of profoundly mentally handicapped children.* Jordanhill College of Education.

Goldenberg, P (1979). *Special Technology for Special Children: Computers to serve communication and autonomy in the education of handicapped children.* University Press.

Goldenberg, P *et al.* (1984). *Computers, Education and Special Needs.* Addison-Wesley Publishing Company.

Millar, S M, Nisbet, P D, Odor, J P, with Milne, M. *Communication Aids and Computer Based Learning: Assessment Techniques and Related developments for Communication Impaired Learners.* Call Centre, Edinburgh University.

Rostron, A & Sewell, D (1983). *Microtechnology in Special Education .* Croom Helm.

Sigel, I E (1979). *Infants at Risk: Assessment of Cognitive Functioning.* Lawrence Erlbaum.

Resources

CALL Centre, Dept of Education, University of Edinburgh, 4 Buccleuch Place, Edinburgh EH8 9JT.

Functional Visual Assessment Package, M Buultjens, Moray House College of Education, Holyrood Road, Edinburgh.

Manufacturers/Suppliers

Ref 1.	QED (Quest Educational Designs), 1 Prince Alfred Street, Gosport, Hants, PO12 1QH.
Ref 2.	TFH (Toys for the Handicapped), 76 Barracks Road, Sandy Lane Industrial Estate, Stourport-on-Severn, Worcs, DY13 9QB.
Ref 3.	Brilliant Computing P O Box 142, Bradford, BD3 0JN.
Ref 4.	Liberator Ltd., Whitegates, Lincs, NG33 4PA.
Ref 5.	Kirton Liteworks Ltd., Unit 2, Woodgate Park, Whitelund Industrial Estate, Morecambe, LA3 3PS.

Developing Communication through Interaction

Christine Knight

Introduction
This article is primarily concerned with the development of communication in pupils with severe and profound learning difficulties. In particular it looks at the natural model of communication, and how this model can be applied to pupils who are at very early stages of development.

Early development - the natural model
There is clear evidence in the literature from the study of normal development that communication develops through interaction. Wells (1981) describes his view that the development of communication is 'fundamentally interactional' as follows:

> At each stage, the child endeavours to communicate using the resources currently available to him. The adult with whom he is interacting interprets his behaviour in terms of their cultural and linguistic framework and responds in a way that reflects to the child the perceived significance of his behaviour, and the content of that response provides information about the communication system and its relation to the world that enables the child to supplement and magnify his communicative resources.

What he has observed from extensive research is that through interacting with adults, children do not only learn the external behaviours that make up communication, but begin to understand the underlying processes which are crucial to becoming effective communicators.

Wells is making a general statement which encompasses pre-verbal and verbal development. Literature on very early development, the first year, confirms the importance of an interactive process between the primary carer and the infant. They are partners in the development process. Trevarthen (1979) emphasises that the baby is an active partner in the communicative exchanges between an infant and his/her carer. His studies of mother-infant pairs have led him to believe that a 'complex form of mutual understanding develops even at this age (2 months). It is both naturally accepted and strongly regulated by the infant. Two month olds exhibit many different experiences, some highly emotional, and they make a variety of attempts to gain the lead in an exchange with another person'.

In typical infant-carer interaction routines the infant brings a range of experiences, sounds, movements, and gestures, and an innate sociability which drives him/her to seek out contact and maintain it with a known adult. The parent comments on, echoes, supports and interprets the baby's behaviour. Through this exchange the baby learns that his/her sounds, actions and movements evoke a reaction in another person, and thus develops initially a sense of self as a separate being, and then an understanding of the idea of communication as a two-way process.

Stern (1977) describes the process as a 'dance' with each participant effortlessly and fluently slipping into the role of initiator, then respondent. The process is maintained through mutual enjoyment, unless there is interruption due to circumstances, such as severe depression, affecting the mother (Murray & Trevarthen, 1985) or the infant. It normally proceeds through age related steps that seem to be universal and essential to normal socialisation and to normal cognitive growth. At each stage new games and routines are evolved, and the parent quickly notices any developments which can be elaborated to help the infant extend onto the next stages.

Relevance of natural model for pupils with severe learning difficulties

This knowledge about normal development has not been widely used in the development of communication with pupils with severe and profound learning difficulties. It is acknowledged in Rectory Paddock School's 'In search of a curriculum' (1988) but not developed as a methodology. Leeming *et al.* (1979), in one of their case histories, list all the ways Susan does communicate, as interpreted by her teacher, but then propose a training programme which does not incorporate any of these. Other texts analyse the steps the infant goes through (e.g. seeking and maintaining eye contact, looking at objects, eye-tracking), but then suggest programmes to train pupils in the behaviours, rather than the eliciting of these important skills through natural interaction. In school settings the emphasis in always on aims, whereas in natural interaction the process is what is important, and developments grow out of the interaction.

Recent work has shown that the infant-carer model does have a lot to offer those working with pupils with profound communication difficulties. Burford (1986) in her role as movement therapist developed this approach, and has more recently studied in depth what produces the most effective communication between young people with profound learning difficulties and their carers. Her video (1990), demonstrates a variety of adults, parents, relatives and carers using exactly the style of interaction described between infants and carers. They observe, interpret and respond. They invent games which captivate the interest; they follow the young person's lead; they emphasise with their movement, and allow him/her to control the interaction. Hewett and Nind (1989) have also used this model and developed a process-based curriculum at a school working primarily with young mentally-handicapped adults in a long-stay institution. Through contact with the work of both Burford, and Hewett & Nind, an interactive curriculum has been developed at Gogarburn School.

As in many schools for pupils with profound learning difficulties, natural and often playful interactions between staff and pupils took place throughout the day, but were not seen as the focus for intensive development. Communication programmes were written for pupils emphasising the need for pre-linguistic skills such as eye-contact, turn taking, joint attention, but they were taught in a structured situation through behaviourist techniques, or through structured games.

Intensive interaction was introduced as a central part of the curriculum because staff seemed intuitively aware that it had a lot to offer our pupils. We used the term 'intensive interaction', coined by Nind and Hewett (1988), because it seemed to emphasise what we felt were crucial aspects. It stressed the importance of the interaction, but it also emphasised that to be a valid part of the curriculum it has to be more focused than the kind of spontaneous interactions we were used to. This meant time-tabled individual sessions for most pupils. A full description of the implementation, staff development, and evaluation of intensive interaction at Gogarburn School is available from Moray House College. (Knight and Watson, 1990). Although initially piloted at Gogarburn School, it is now established in the curriculum of a number of schools for pupils with severe and profound learning difficulties in Lothian Region and Fife. It is firmly entrenched in developmental theory, but adapted to be an appropriate part of the curriculum in an educational setting.

In a one-to-one setting staff member and pupil engage in the kind of interactional flow described as characterising early infant interaction. Like the infant, the pupil brings a range of movements, vocalisations, expressions, gestures and sometimes stereotyped behaviours. The staff member during an intensive interaction session does not attempt to modify behaviours, or even particularly to reward behaviours. She accepts what the pupil is bringing to the session, and engages in an equal way. As the carers do with the infant, the staff member enjoys, comments on, sometimes enlarges on, or gives exaggerated response to a pupil's behaviour. He/she is constantly interpreting the behaviour as meaningful and constructive. This may mean feeding back verbally, or it may entail a physical response. In all natural interactions there is shared control, and sometimes the pupil leads the 'dance', sometimes the adult. Mutual enjoyment is fundamental as this, rather than any external reward, is what maintains the interactions. A full description of the elements which may be part of interactions is available in Nind and Hewett (1988).

Staff reactions to the use of intensive interaction vary. Some feel threatened

- they are anxious that they won't know what to 'do'. They have perhaps come to rely heavily on structured teaching situations, but doubtful staff are often pleasantly surprised when they participate in sessions. Many, both sceptics and enthusiasts, have commented that they feel they know a pupil much better when they engage in intensive interaction. This has been said about pupils with whom they have been working for many years. Focusing on the whole person, rather than on a task, being with someone rather than trying to lead them through a routine, spending time observing and watching even through long minutes of inactivity, all seem to contribute to their knowledge. Staff also report moments of engagement when they absolutely know that someone is aware of their presence, and is communicating directly with them. There is a quality of engagement described which no quantitative measurement of 'seconds of eye contact' can fully describe.

Although the model used in interaction is the infant-carer model, there are many ways in which intensive interaction differs. In the early weeks and months a baby is tremendously responsive, changing daily, and it seems, strongly motivated to seek out human interaction. The parent is totally involved with this tiny new person and every slight change is noted and celebrated. The parents or carers are in the presence of the infant most of its waking hours, and there develops a rhythm of sleep, feeding and activity which fits into the daily life of the family. Interactions therefore always take place in a natural setting, when the infant is in the optimum condition - fed, rested and in a state of suitable arousal.

In a school setting many of the young people with severe and profound learning difficulties are not at all motivated to seek social contact. For some this is symptomatic of their learning difficulties (e.g. pupils with autism); for others, it may be that they have, in the past, had so little feedback for their attempts at communication that they have become disaffected and very passive or self-stimulatory. They have perhaps been unable to develop a sense of themselves as separate beings, which as we have seen, is a function of interaction in early infancy. Others develop more extreme ways of attempting to communicate which are then construed as unacceptable behaviour and deliberately ignored or punished. For these reasons many of these pupils are going to be harder to reach than a sociable, responsive baby.

The age and size of pupils also makes interaction more difficult with some of the older profoundly handicapped pupils. Few of us fail to respond in delight to a baby's sounds and movements, but it is undoubtedly harder to maintain that sort of interest and enthusiasm with young people who change very slowly, and whose repertoire of behaviour is very limited. It is also more difficult to handle older physically disabled pupils in the way one might an infant e.g. rocking, bumping up and down. It is very important to note, in relation to age, that although this model is based on early interaction, it is not treating people like babies. The skills used by carers are observed and developed, but adapted for use with older pupils, to show respect for chronological age.

Although I emphasise the open-endedness of the interaction, in contrast to having specific aims, it is important that it is seen as part of an educational programme. This means that although spontaneous interactions should be encouraged and enjoyed there also has to be a focused, time-tabled session for each pupil which is recorded.

Evaluations of progress and new developments must be made regularly. The staff member taking part in a session is using a natural model, but is informed of the theory behind it, and has detailed information on the pupil's communication skills. She will therefore know where possible developments would be, and while still being interactive in style will attempt to help the pupil move on. For staff, intensive interaction requires a depth of knowledge of development, careful planning, recording and evaluating, plus creativity, opportunity and a sense of fun. It is certainly no easy option for staff.

The applications of intensive interaction

Initially it seems that intensive interaction is most appropriate for pupils with profound learning difficulties who are functioning at very early levels of development. There has been notable success with these pupils, particularly noticeable in those who have not had one consistent carer in their life to provide this input. Tracy is one pupil, resident as a long stay pupil, who has benefited in this way.

Tracy's story

Tracy is multiply handicapped, almost blind, and has very little mobility. EV is the nursery nurse who works with her, and has known her for many years in the special care unit of the hospital. EV finds interaction with Tracy especially rewarding as Tracy shows she enjoys social contact and is particularly responsive during these sessions, though she is a child who is prone to dropping off to sleep in many situations. EV engages Tracy in typical mother-child 'games' during interaction, rhythmical rocking, cradling her, whispering, tapping her hands, successfully attempting to make Tracy lift her head, and is able to elicit laughter by varying the timing of her actions. EV talks to Tracy a lot, and Tracy responds with variations in her breathing, throaty noises, smiles and laughter, and occasionally thrashes out her legs in an excited manner. During the first three sessions there was some evidence that Tracy was controlling her head better than usual. A toy shaker held near her face and tipped rhythmically by EV resulted in apparent alertness, a still, interested expression. Session IV saw the introduction of a small compressible squeaky rubber caterpillar by EV, who skilfully enabled Tracy to make it sound by her own head movements, four times within a minute. During Session V, EV used the same toy with Tracy during almost the whole of an exceptionally long and successful period of interaction. This fifth session was remarkable for the sustained level of interest and activity shown by Tracy. Tracy was seen to be developing an appreciation of cause and effect relationships, involving objects, already apparent in the way she anticipates EV's actions in rhythmic repetitive games. (Knight and Watson, 1990)

Pupils who have developed some speech or signing are often not considered suitable for intensive interaction sessions. They are often taught in more formal settings where they concentrate on learning to name objects, or to learn signs for objects. Yet all communication is learned through interaction. Wells has studied communication development up to the age of five and concluded that although adults certainly feed in vocabulary as appropriate, the child learns about total communication through joint activities where the focus is not on learning language.

Bruner (1983) has studied in detail the acquisition of communication skills and comments:

The development of language, then, involves two people negotiating. Language is not encountered willy-nilly by the child, it is shaped to make communicative interaction effective - fine-tuned.

He suggests that adults adapt their speech to take account of the child's grasp of conceptual distinctions and communicative functions, and through familiar and routine games and tasks, highlight the significant features of communication or language which the child needs to grasp. The pattern is very similar to what was described earlier as evolving between infants and carers, but with the introduction of language. Yet many teachers in special education take a didactic approach to teaching communication using material which concentrates on naming objects and activities, and responding to linguistic demands.

Harris (1988) looked in detail at how staff in special schools teach communication, and concluded that teachers end up using very structured approaches, partly because research in the field advocates a behavioural approach, but also because it is easier for teachers to plan programmes, break down skills and teach them when they concentrate on the observable features of communication such as naming objects. The teachers who responded to his questionnaire did however acknowledge that language was developed through all their activities, not just those set up to 'teach' language. According to Bruner's model, they can actually learn more about communication through other activities than through direct teaching, particularly if the language input to the activities is 'fine-tuned' to the child's conceptual level.

Harris advocates the use of the natural model and suggest that teachers should consider 'the design of classroom activities which enhance these processes underlying the acquisition of language'. I would suggest that using intensive interaction does this. Although it may initially seem very demanding in that a teacher cannot possibly interact with every child in the way a parent would at home, in practice it is not impossible.

Many children have regular individual sessions with a teacher or speech therapist where they are required to follow structured programmes, or they engage in question and answer routines. These do not have communicative functions for the pupil; he/she merely learns an external behaviour, pointing, or naming an object which is then rewarded by the teacher. Without any alteration in resources the same session can be used for interactive play, where the same principles as described for intensive interaction apply. The games must involve a two-way process, power must be shared so that the child and the adult are equal partners, and the activity must be maintained by mutual enjoyment.

It may involve rough and tumble play, running and chasing games outside or in the swimming pool, routine and pretend play with objects, or pretend play (e.g. being a dog). The staff member responds to the pupil's communication in a meaningful way and purposefully waits for initiations from the pupil.

Many games and activities developed for pupils beginning to use language do have interactive aspects e.g. music activities and group games, but there is also a place for the more open-ended intensive interaction approach. Many pupils with severe learning difficulties become very passive communicators, responding only to direct questions and with prompts. Empowering pupils to be active, developing their own games and leading adults through play routines can help them grasp the processes of communication and so use them more effectively.

Jon's story

Jon is a five year old in an assessment nursery who will go to a school for pupils with severe learning difficulties. He has some speech, single words and phrases which he uses intermittently, and often in stereotypical fashion. In his second year in the nursery, the staff have found him disinterested, limited in his play to one or two objects, and unwilling to be drawn into activities by staff or other children. He is not disruptive but always says "no" when asked to do something, and spends long periods lying on the floor. It was suggested he would benefit from intensive interaction, and he took part in four sessions with me, in the PE hall, and has subsequently continued these sessions with the speech therapist.

In the first session we engaged in some rough and tumble play. He pushed me and I fell over with exaggerated fall and verbal response. He laughed delightedly and this game continued and others developed, involving similar activities. He soon realised that he could direct me and a kind of follow the leader developed. He used some language - all of it appropriate. In the second session a large portion of the time was taken up with moving around large pieces of soft play equipment. He did not involve me deliberately but responded to my initiations when I climbed into the circular piece. He talked to himself, and sometimes to me about what he was doing, and began to incorporate my verbal responses into his narration e.g. I said "up" when we lifted something up, and "down" when it fell, and he later repeated this appropriately.

The third and fourth sessions developed into imaginative play, involving lots of movement, and were clearly enjoyed enormously by him. He initiated almost all the games, and I responded either by joining in with him, or adopting another appropriate role. He pretended to be a giant, a tiger, and a ghost, each time showing a remarkably sophisticated level of observation and interpretation. Again, he commented verbally on what was going on, and incorporated my comments appropriately e.g. "backwards" and "forwards" when we were running up and down the hall.

Jon showed a side of himself in the sessions that had not been seen in the nursery setting. He was completely different from the rather negative little boy experienced by his teacher. The freedom of the hall, with no focus on toys or equipment, and the equality of the relationship between us, the power-sharing, enabled Jon to develop his natural imaginative play and allowed him to develop his communication through joining him in his play. The speech therapist who had been seeing him for a year in the classroom was delighted with what she experienced in the interaction sessions. What he developed in early sessions with me, he had no difficulty in transferring to her. It is too early to see if the sessions will help his development in the classroom setting.

A third group of pupils are those with very challenging behaviour. For many of these pupils their behaviour is a form of communication. They have not found positive ways to communicate effectively, and often use their behaviour to avoid social interaction altogether. McGee *et al.* (1987) suggest that many people with severe learning difficulties and challenging behaviour need to learn the benefits of positive social interaction. This is not easy in situations where the focus of the interaction is a task that the adult wants the child to do. Intensive interaction has proved a very effective way of reaching and being with such individuals. This does not mean allowing them to do what they want, tolerating dangerous or threatening behaviour, or running behind them trying to join in their destructive behaviour. It means taking time in a safe environment, a quiet room, to be with the pupil, to look for and respond to any initiation from him/her, and to demonstrate caring and positive regard by showing empathy, by reflecting their physical stance and movement, accepting their behaviours as meaningful, for example stereotypical rocking or pacing, joining in with this or making other appropriate physical responses. These are some of the ways staff have responded to such pupils, and report very positive enhancement of relationships.

Interactive learning

This article is primarily about developing communication through interaction, but I would like to conclude with some general remarks about what makes good learning experiences in any situation. I have done a number of workshops with teachers which have looked at their own learning experiences as adults. Some interesting and lively discussions have led to some general points about what contributes to effective learning. While recognising that in some situations like studying for an Open University degree to enhance career prospects, individualised learning with extrinsic motivation is effective, most people found that feeling some power in the learning situation (shared control), enjoying the actual learning experience for itself (intrinsic motivation), and feeling that the teacher appreciated what they could do already and helped them to discover the next step in the process (particularly in practical activities), were the kinds of factors that helped them learn with enjoyment and confidence. Being allowed to make mistakes and correct them and try different ways of doing things were also mentioned.

The structure of schools makes it very difficult for learning to take place in this way, but special education with staffing which allows for individualised learning does give the opportunity to take some of these issues on board. Unfortunately, this model of guided discovery has been rejected by many educationalists in favour of the skills analysis model. Gardner *et al.* (1983) firmly reject developmental models as being inappropriate for people with learning difficulties, and suggest that a curriculum should describe 'the observable behaviour of the student rather than any inferred process'. The literature on communication development shows clearly that the underlying processes are of paramount importance and I would argue that this is also true in other areas of learning. Task analysis, small steps through a hierarchy of skills, prompting and so on, do not allow for any learning through getting it wrong, or attempting a task in a number of different ways. This approach allows no shared control, motivation is extrinsic and rewards are often of dubious value to the student. Many important teaching skills have been learned through the behaviourist model, such as observation, and breaking down tasks, but as a total model for the curriculum it leaves a lot to be desired.

This is not a new debate. McConkey has been arguing for many years against the product orientated, skills model in favour of discovery through play and activity, and his excellent books and videos (1984, 1986) give a very clear model for interactive learning. Smith (1986, 1987) also raises these issues. During the nineteen seventies Stevens advocated a very broad approach which looked at the whole child and advocated interaction as opposed to concentrating on tasks and skills (1976).

In the area of severe learning difficulties there has been too much emphasis on observable skills and behaviour. I would argue that we should be looking for ways of helping young people become more active partners in the learning process not only in the development of communication but also in the broader curriculum. Intensive interaction demonstrates how this can be done, in one area, with considerable success.

References

Bruner, J (1983). *Child's Talk.* Oxford University Press.

Burford, B (1986). Communication through Movement. In Shanley, E (ed). *Mental Handicap: a handbook of care.* Churchill Livingstone.

Burford, B (1990). *Children with Profound Handicaps: how carers can communicate.* Video and booklet Health Promotion Trust.

Gardner, J *et al.* (1983). *The Skills Analysis Model.* BIMH.

Harris, J (1988). *Language Development in Schools for Children with Severe Learning Difficulties.* Croom Helm.

Knight, C & Watson, J (1990). *Intensive Interactive teaching at Gogarburn School.* Moray House College, Edinburgh.

Leeming, K *et al.* (1979). *Teaching Language and Communication to the mentally handicapped.* Evans/Methuen Educational.

McConkey, R & Gallagher, F (1984). *Let's Play.* University of Ulster.

McConkey, R & Price, P (1986). *Let's Talk.* Souvenir.

McGee, J *et al.* (1987). *Gentle Teaching.* Human Sciences Press.

Murray, L & Trevarthen, C (1985). Emotional regulations of interactions between two-month-olds and their mothers. In Field, T M (ed), *Social Perception in Infants.* Norwood.

Nind, M & Hewett, D (1988). Interaction as Curriculum. *B J spec ed* 15,2.

Rectory Paddock School (1988). *In search of a curriculum.* Robin Wren.

Smith, B *et al.* (1983). Education with Understanding? *Special Education: Forward Trends,* 10 (2).

Smith, B (ed). (1987). *Interactive Approaches to the Education of Children with Severe Learning Difficulties.* Westhill College, Birmingham.

Stevens, M (1976). *The Educational and Social Needs of children with severe handicap.* Edward Arnold.

Stern, D (1971). *The First Relationship: Infant and Mother.* Fontana.

Trevarthen, C (1979). Communication and cooperation in early infancy: a description of primary intersubjectivity. In Bullowa, M (ed). *Before Speech.* Cambridge University Press.

Wells, G (1987). *Learning through Interaction.* Cambridge University Press.

A Functional Communication Approach

Anne Edmonstone

Introduction

It is only in recent years that speech and language therapists have become involved in working with children with very severe learning difficulties. The role of the speech and language therapist within such schools is one that varies from school to school, and even from class to class. Usually, the speech and language therapist has a limited amount of time to spend in the school. Harris (1988) in a survey of ESN (S) schools in Wales found that on average speech therapists visited two half days per week. She/he therefore has to devise realistic ways of working, which will maximise his/her input, and yet are based on sound theoretical perspectives.

Typically, children with very severe learning difficulties present with little or no speech. Leeming, Swann, Coupe and Mittler (1978), in a study of ESN (S) schools in Manchester and Cheshire found that approximately one third of the children were at or below the level of imitating single words. Children with very severe learning difficulties are also likely to have poorly developed interaction skills and additionally sensory and motor handicaps (Hewett and Nind, 1987).

The speech and language therapist works as part of the school team. Gone are the days when he/she worked in a little room, withdrawing children individually for half an hour once a week. Roulstone (1986) has discussed why this is not an effective method of intervention. She argues that 'the speech therapist who operates entirely in withdrawal rooms is ignoring factors in the environment which are fundamentally related to the child's success as a communicator'. There is still a place for individual therapy, but this can only be effective where a key-worker from the classroom is involved, so that the key-worker can continue the therapy at times when the therapist is not available.

Ideally, the speech and language therapist will be actively involved in the development of the communication curriculum of the school. Such a curriculum will encompass the provision of a communicatively stimulating environment, where the children are provided with opportunities to make choices, to reject and refuse, and to initiate communication (Coupe and Goldbart, 1988). In addition, the speech and language therapist should have the opportunity to contribute to the joint planning of the pupil's individual educational programmes (Cospen, 1984). The speech and language therapist has a considerable part to play in the treatment of the eating and drinking problems which occur in many pupils with severe learning difficulties, and together with the occupational therapist and physiotherapist will be involved in devising feeding programmes (Anderson, 1983).

However, in the assessment and treatment of communication disorders lie the particular skills of the speech and language therapist.

Assessment

The assessment of the communication skills of children with severe learning difficulties will be ongoing. It is only through observing the child in various communicative settings, and with a variety of communication partners, that an accurate assessment can be made.

Assessments such as the Pre-Verbal Communication Schedule (Kiernan and Reid, 1987), the Affective Communication Assessment (Coupe, Barber and Murphy, 1988) and the Pragmatic Profile (Dewart and Summers, 1988) are useful tools. In addition to these, the speech and language therapist will usually devise his/her own assessment which will aim at providing the pupil with activities which will assist the therapist to assess pre-linguistic skills, symbolic functioning, play and language abilities.

Therapy

Where, and how and with whom the speech and language therapist works is very much a matter for negotiation between the individual teacher and the therapist. This will depend on the children in the class and how the teacher perceives the role of the speech and language therapist.

The speech and language therapist has skills to offer in the areas of:

1. Intensive interaction therapy (Hewitt and Nind, 1987, Knight, this volume).

2. The development of pre-linguistic skills and symbolic functioning.

3. The development of alternative and augmentative systems of communication (symbol systems, signing systems, low-tech and high-tech communication aids).

4. The development of language skills, through the use of scripted joint-action routines (Nelson, 1985, Snyder-McLean, *et al.*, 1984).

Often, however, the speech and language therapist has to prioritise his/her input because of time limitations. One way of doing this is for the speech and language therapist to provide additional activities in the school timetable which are specifically designed to facilitate communication. Such activities are sometimes called Functional Communication Groups.

The functional communication group

Language learning research in recent years which has been based on the development of first meanings provides a useful framework for activities aimed at developing the communication skills of children with very severe learning difficulties. Halliday (1975) described how 'a child who is learning his first language is learning how to mean'. He argues that 'the learning of language is essentially the learning of a semantic system, and this process is already well under way before the child has any words at all'. It seems therefore that this approach can appropriately be applied to children with very severe learning difficulties who have few or no words. It was Halliday who called this a *functional approach* because 'the child learns language as a system of meanings in *functional contexts*'. The aim, therefore, of the functional communication group is to provide situations where the children can learn first meanings in a functional or meaningful way.

Halliday identified 6 functions in the development of communication in the young child.

Instrumental	-	satisfying needs
Regulatory	-	controlling the behaviours of others
Interactional	-	"me and you" functions of language, greetings, names
Personal	-	awareness of self
Heuristic	-	questioning, seeking information
Imaginative	-	let's pretend

Bloom and Lahey (1978) identified 12 meanings that young children communicate.

Existence	-	child indicates that object exists (name, this)
Nonexistence	-	child indicates that the object is not where he expects it to be
Disappearance	-	child indicates that something/someone has disappeared
Recurrence	-	child indicates that he wants more
Action	-	child communicates about an action e.g. go, get
Attribute	-	child describes object or person
Denial	-	child denies doing something
Agent	-	person or object that performs action
Object	-	person or object affected by action
Possession	-	child indicates to whom object belongs

Coupe, Barton and Walker (1988) have described a method of teaching first meanings in a structured way. This is very similar to the approach described here, with communication games used to teach first meanings.

The ideal size of a functional communication group is around six with the speech therapist, teachers and nursery nurses or classroom assistants working as a team and responding to any attempts at communication by members of the group, be they verbal or non-verbal. Usually the group will consist of the entire class. Often such groups will be of mixed ability. This is useful because it means that the more able children can be encouraged to interact with the less able children. More able children can be presented with more complex tasks. There are broad communication aims for the group, in addition to individual aims for each child within the group. Although the primary aim is to teach first meanings, the activities are such that there are opportunities for developing the non-verbal and language skills which are necessary for effective communication. For example, the group aim may be to teach the meanings of disappearance and recurrence, through hiding a ball, but at the same time the other skills involved will include object permanence, joint attention, visual tracking, turn-taking and anticipation.

These groups also incorporate the interactional principles described by Knight, who has identified four main features of successful interaction:

two way process
responsiveness
shared control
mutual enjoyment.

The role of the professionals in the functional communication group should be similar to that of the carer in an interactional group and should exhibit:

adaptability
exaggeration
initiation
transfer of emotion
turn-taking
responsiveness.

In addition to being a learning experience, functional communication groups should be fun - many of the activities are based on party games. The way in which the activities are carried out depends very much on the personalities and sensitivity of the staff involved.

The activities and games used during functional communication groups follow a fairly predictable structure, so that the children become familiar with the sequence of events within the game. Nelson (1986) has suggested that children organise their understanding of familiar activities in terms of *general event representations*. She argues that such scripts facilitate the development of communication, by providing a common linguistic context for the adult and child, thus enabling the adult and child to understand each other's utterances. In addition, Nelson also suggests that as the child becomes familiar with the script he is able to concentrate more on the language involved and less on the activity.

Once the children have become familiar with the routine of the game, the staff begin to employ strategies to encourage initiation by the children. Such strategies usually involve changing the routine or making deliberate mistakes like missing someone out, doing something silly or wrong or pretending not to notice something. These 'mistakes' not only increase the children's enjoyment of the game, but also are very effective in stimulating communication.

Activities for functional communication groups

Most of these games can be adapted to accommodate the abilities of the children involved. Each activity will teach a range of first meanings. However, the meanings will often be dependent upon how the therapist carries out the activity.

1. Beanbag/Ball Naming. Existence, Action, Agent (Bloom and Lahey), Regulatory, Interactional (Halliday). The group is seated in a circle. Someone in the middle with a beanbag calls a name and throws it to the named person, or without someone in the middle each person names someone and throws the beanbag.

2. Objects in the bag. Existence, Action, Object (Bloom and Lahey), Regulatory, Imaginative (Halliday). Each child must put their hand in a bag and choose an object. Once they have chosen the object it can be named and used appropriately, e.g. brush, brush hair. **Song** "This is the way we brush our hair" (to the tune of 'The Mulberry Bush').

3. Hat and Scarf Game. Existence, Action, Object, Agent (Bloom and Lahey), Interactional (Halliday). Bag of hats and scarfs. Each child chooses an item of clothing and everyone sings "Michael's got a hat on" to the tune of 'The sun has got his hat on'.

4. Pass the Parcel. Existence, (Bloom and Lahey), Regulatory, Interactional (Halliday). Sit in a circle. When the music stops, unwrap the parcel. It is better to have a selection of parcels, each with one layer of paper.

5. Musical Bumps. Existence, Action, Agent (Bloom and Lahey), Regulatory, Interactional, Personal (Halliday). Dance to music or use a musical instrument such as a drum or a tambourine. When the music stops, everyone must sit down.

6. Musical Statues. Existence, Action, Agent, Object (Bloom and Lahey), Regulatory, Interactional, Personal (Halliday). Walk round to music or use a musical instrument such as a drum or a tambourine. When the music stops, everyone must stop walking. A child can bang the drum and shout "stop".

7. Races. Action, Agent (Bloom and Lahey), Regulatory, Interactional (Halliday). Any kinds of races, forwards, backwards, jumping, crawling. All the competitors have to listen for "ready, steady, GO" before they start. A child can say "GO".

Hiding Games. Existence, Nonexistence, Disappearance, Recurrence (Bloom and Lahey), Regulatory, Interactional, (Halliday).

8. Hide the Ball. Hide a ball (up your jumper, behind someone, under a chair) and see if someone can find it. Or **Ali-Bali Who's got the ball?** Someone hides the ball on their person and everyone says "Ali-Bali who's got the ball? I haven't got it, in my pocket. Ali-Bali who's got the ball?"

9. Hide the person/Hide and seek. Throw a cover over someone and then ask: "Where's John?" or "Who's hiding?" This can develop into peek-a-boo. Or take someone out of the room and see if the others know who's gone, or take two people out of the room and bring one back hidden under a sheet. Gradually uncover that person, starting with feet and hands, until children know who it is.

10. Blind-Man's Bluff. Blindfold someone and see if they can recognise who they are feeling.

11. Hide-and-seek. Even less able physically handicapped children enjoy this. They and their wheelchair can be hidden. Encourage them to vocalise in response to "Where's Susan?" More able children must follow instructions as to where to hide, e.g. under the table.

12. Hiding the Sweet. Hide a sweet in one hand, hide your hands behind your back, see if someone can remember and tell you which hand it is in.

13. Sweet-in-the-Tin. Use two identical tins, one containing sweets. Shake them both and see if the child can find the sweets.

14. Treasure Hunt. Hide small objects around the room and see who can find them.

15. Find the legs. Lie everyone except one child in the group on the floor and cover them with a sheet, with only their legs showing. Ask the child to find someone's legs e.g. "Find Simon's Legs".

16. Copying Gross Movements. Action, Agent (Bloom and Lahey), Regulatory, Personal (Halliday). All stand in a circle. The group copy the movements of one person. This can be a member of staff or one of the children e.g. jumping, waving arms.

17. Obeying Oral Commands. Action, Agent (Bloom and Lahey), Regulatory, Personal (Halliday). Everyone has to follow spoken commands:- e.g. "Everyone Jump".

18. Forfeits. Existence, Possession (Bloom and Lahey), Regulatory, Personal, Heuristic (Halliday). **Whose is this Shoe?** All take off a shoe, or an item of clothing. Hold up a shoe and say "Whose is this shoe?" Making mistakes encourages communication.

19. The clothes game. Existence, Denial, Object (Bloom and Lahey), Regulatory, Interactional, Personal (Halliday). Use a bag of clothes and get the children to tell/show you where you wear each item of clothing. Make mistakes, putting clothes on the wrong part of your body.

20. Ten in the bed. Existence, Recurrence, Action, Agent (Bloom and Lahey), Regulatory, Interactional, Personal (Halliday). Everyone squashed onto a sofa, bed or row of chairs. Sing "Ten in the bed", naming each person as they fall out.

21. Lazy Katie. Existence, Action, Denial, Agent (Bloom and Lahey), Regulatory, Interactional, Personal, Imaginative (Halliday). One child lies on the floor with a blanket. Staff sing: "Lazy Katie will you get out of bed, get out of bed, get out of bed, Lazy Katie will you get out of bed on a Wednesday morning", (to the tune of Mulberry Bush). Child has to indicate "yes" or "no". Staff choose something to give child or to do to child. Staff sing: "If we tickle you hard will you get out of bed," or "If we give you a crisp will you get out of bed?" Child indicates "yes" or "no", if she says "no" she is tickled.

22. Body parts game. Existence, Action, Object, Agent (Bloom and Lahey), Regulatory, Interactional (Halliday). One child or member of staff stands in the middle of the group. Each child is given a bright sticky label and is told to stick it on a part of the model's body. e.g. "Stick it on her tummy". To make this more complicated, you can ask the children to stick on different people. e.g. "Stick it on Peter's leg". Or, choose where you want to stick it.

23. Lucky Dip. Existence, Nonexistence, Disappearance, Object (Bloom and Lahey) Instrumental, Regulatory, Heuristic (Halliday). Attach lengths of string to favourite toys or musical instruments. Put them in a box with the strings exposed. Children have to pull a string to choose a toy. Or hide toys in sand box or in sawdust, children must find them.

24. Use of a Voice Output Communication Aid. A voice output communication aid such as the Introtalker can be used effectively during functional communication groups. By programming it with the relevant language it can be used to allow children to be more active communicators in all the games previously described and to use the machine in a meaningful way. It can be programmed with songs and appropriate objects or pictures may be placed on the corresponding squares of the machine. E.g. a toy dog on one square when pressed causes the machine to emit "How much is that doggy in the window?" Different animal noises may be produced by touching toy animals on the machine, or children can make choices by touching the object or a square causing the machine to say the object's name. Photographs of the children in the group can be put on the machine. Children choose who they will sing to, sit beside, or give something to.

Conclusion

The functional communication group is one way that the speech and language therapist can provide activities which are theoretically based and are aimed at developing the communication skills of children with very severe learning difficulties.

References

Anderson, C A (1983). *Feeding - A Guide to Assessment and Intervention with Handicapped Children*. Jordanhill College of Education.

Bloom, L and Lahey, M (1978). *Language Development and Language Disorders*. John Wiley.

Bruner, J (1983). *Child's talk: learning to use language*. Oxford University Press.

Cospen (1984). *Learning Together*. Scottish Consultative Committee on the Curriculum, Edinburgh.

Coupe, J, Barber, M and Murphy, D (1988). *Affective Communication*. In Coupe, J and Goldbart, J (eds), *Communication Before Speech*, Croom Helm.

Coupe, J. Barton, L and Walker, S (1988). *Teaching First Meaning*. In Coupe, J and Goldbart, J (eds). *Communication before Speech*. Croom Helm.

Coupe, J and Porter, J (eds). (1986). *The Education of Children with Severe Learning Difficulties*. Croom Helm.

Dewart, H and Summers, S (1988). *Pragmatics Profile of Early Communication Skills*. NFER - Nelson.

Goldbart, J (1986). *The Development of Language and Communication*. In Coupe, J and Porter, J (eds). *The Education of Children with Severe Learning Difficulties*. Croom Helm.

Halliday, M. (1975). *Learning how to mean - Explorations in the Development of Language*. Arnold.

Harris, J (1988). *Language Development in Schools for Children with Severe Learning Difficulties*. Croom Helm.

Hewitt, D and Nind, M (1987). Developing an Interactive Curriculum for Pupils with Severe and Complex Learning Difficulties: A Classroom Process. In Smith, B (ed). *Interactive Approaches to the Education of Children with Severe Learning Difficulties*. Westhill College, Birmingham.

Kiernan, C and Reid, B (1987). *The Pre-verbal Communication Schedule*. (PVCS) NFER - Nelson.

Leeming, K, Swann, W, Coupe, J and Mittler, P (1979). *Teaching Language and Communication to the Mentally Handicapped*. Evans/Methuen Educational.

Nelson, K (ed). (1986). *Event Knowledge: Structure and Function in Development*. Lawrence Erlbaum Associates.

Schaffer, H R (1979). *Early Interaction Development*. In Oates, J (ed). *Early Cognitive Development*. OU Press/Croom Helm.

Roulstone, S (1986). *The Speech Therapist*. In Coupe, J and Porter, J (eds). *The Education of Children with Severe Learning Difficulties*. Croom Helm.

Snyder-McLean, L, Solomon, B, McLean, J and Sacks, S (1984). *Structuring joint-action routines: a strategy for facilitating communication and language development in the classroom*. Grune-Stratton.

Recipe Reading Project

Margaret Mackay and Maureen Lorimer

Introduction

The recipe reading project started in an attempt to give meaningful expression to the small word recognition abilities of three young teenagers, with severe learning difficulties, attending a small special school in Fife Region.

This article will examine the background to the development of the recipe reading project, outline the long term aims, describe the content of the programmes and illustrate extensions to the project. An evaluation will be made and possible future developments discussed.

Background

The perception of the teaching of reading as an integral component of the teacher's role, coupled with parental expectations (and sometimes misconceptions) heightens the need to resolve the uncertainties and anxieties facing teachers of pupils with severe learning difficulties who wish to develop word recognition skills. In the absence of traditional practice to guide teachers a dilemma exists as to how best to adapt teaching materials and methods used at the infant stage to meet the special educational needs of pupils who are much more mature in terms of chronological age.

In 1984 several main approaches were in evidence in the teaching of reading to teenagers and young adults with severe learning difficulties. The first relied upon the use of standard well respected reading schemes such as Link-Up, (Reid 1973); the second focused upon a Social Sight vocabulary approach which had been regarded by many as a means of resolving the difficulty. A third possibility existed in exploring basic but more age-appropriate reading materials utilised by the Learning Support Service, and a fourth in capitalising upon pupil interest and knowledge by creating individual vocabulary banks based upon the pupil's family, friends and personal activities.

a. Infant Reading Schemes. While it can be assumed that most young primary pupils will progress from the foundation provided by infant readers to more advanced forms of reading utilising learned strategies, for pupils with severe learning difficulties this is an assumption which cannot be made and two main implications result from their slower rate of development. Firstly their initial introduction even to the most basic pre-formal reading activities may be considerably delayed and subsequently there is every likelihood that an entire school career will be spent mastering the early stages contained in infant readers, leading to the undignified spectacle of teenagers labouring over books depicting children aged 5 and 6. This unsatisfactory situation is compounded by the fact that the words learned have no immediate functional value to these young adults.

b. Social Sight Vocabulary. A focus on Social Sight vocabulary appears to answer many of the requirements of teachers educating pupils with severe learning difficulties. It is age appropriate, practical, and avoids the complexities of teaching pupils to link words together in sentences. Honest appraisal of the future lifestyle of pupils, however, must acknowledge that as only a small minority will be able to negotiate the outside environment independently, constraints are placed on the functional usefulness of the Social Sight Vocabulary programme. While undeniably of value as a component to a word recognition programme, its content is not sufficient to justify its sole adoption.

c. Learning Support Materials. Examination of a variety of materials indicated that while the text of readers is simplified, lifestyles portrayed, which ranged from the adventures of street-wise lads on motorcycles to supremos on the football field, are far removed from the sheltered lives and experiences enforced upon our pupils by the severity of their learning difficulties. This material, however, has been found to be very suitable in promoting listening skills.

d. Personal Wordbanks. This approach is based on techniques formalised in the Breakthrough To Literacy Scheme (1970), but draws core vocabulary from the personal experiences of the individual pupil. Thus, the written word is firmly embedded in a practical context meaningful to the pupil. The potential of this approach has been explored with effective results in work with pupils with moderate learning difficulties in Departments of Special Education within Fife Region. Supported by specially adapted computer disks, the technique has proved motivating to pupils. At the level of severe learning difficulty, given the reduced amount of vocabulary that a pupil may be able to process and retain, it may be necessary to acknowledge limits in terms of the functional application of such learned personal vocabulary. The extent to which the overall approach can be adapted to pupils with severe learning difficulties awaits further exploration.

There appeared, therefore, to be no suitable commercial resources for use in promoting word recognition skills with pupils with severe learning difficulty and it was against this background that we decided to develop a reading programme for a group of three senior pupils which would link to independence skills, particularly cookery. While the recipe reading project focuses on a much narrower aspect of pupil experience in respect of practical cookery skills, it shares many principles and features with the Breakthrough/personal wordbank approach.

Long term aims of recipe reading project

Aims were formulated as follows:

a. To direct whatever small word recognition skills pupils may possess towards a useful and practical end by teaching a small core vocabulary central to following simple recipe instructions.

b. To enable pupils to put individual items of written vocabulary together in a way which is meaningful and linked to a practical end.

c. To maintain high pupil interest in the relatively abstract word recognition component of the project through a visible link to a practical, motivating cookery task with a tangible end product.

d. To enable pupils to take a much more active role in the cookery process, finding out what to do next on their own via number and word recognition, as opposed to relying on prompts for the next stage.

e. To enable pupils to follow through a complete recipe from start to finish, as opposed to carrying out small fragmented parts of a teacher directed task.

f. To provide an instant check on pupil comprehension of the written recipe instruction through observable action by the pupil in the practical situation. It was important to link the written word to real objects and actions from the earliest opportunity to assist in counteracting the mechanical features in reading which have been noted in pupils with severe learning difficulties by their teachers.

g. To promote vital practical independence skills which could be used in future living placements.

h. To enhance cognitive abilities through an accompanying programme of related worksheets, typing activities and computer work.

i. To ultimately provide the pupil with a personal recipe book for future use.

Content of original programme

It should be noted that it was not an aim of the project to enable pupils to read recipes directly out of published recipe books or alternatively to read the abstract instructions on the back of the product labels. It was appreciated that instructions utilising key vocabulary would need to be at the simplest level possible. A whole word approach of the Look and Say variety was used as realistically our pupils had little prospect of mastering letters of the alphabet and phonic strategies. In the case of some basic utensils two words were taught as one phrase in an effort to accelerate progress, for example wooden spoon, milk bottle.

Making packet soup was selected as a starting point and subsequent to the teaching of key vocabulary the following recipe was introduced to the three senior pupils involved in the project:-

Packet soup programme

Bring:
1 the packet
2 the pot
3 the wooden spoon
4 the milk bottle
5 the timer

Instructions:
1 open the packet
2 pour out the powder into the pot
3 fill the milk bottle with cold water
4 pour a little cold water into the pot
5 stir with the wooden spoon
6 pour all the cold water into the pot and stir with the wooden spoon
7 put the pot on the cooker and switch on
8 turn the knob to hi
9 stir the soup until it bubbles
10 turn the knob to 2
11 turn the timer to 5 minutes
12 simmer the soup for 5 minutes
13 turn the knob to off and switch off the cooker
14 take the pot to the table and put the soup into bowls

An analysis of the 36 words forming the core vocabulary of the Packet Soup programme is as follows:-

Key Nouns	Key Verbs	Prepositions	Other
packet	open	into	the
powder	pour	with	a
pot	fill	on	little
milk bottle	stir	to	all
cold water	put	off	and
wooden spoon	switch	for	hi
cooker	turn		until
knob	bubbles		it
soup	simmer		2
timer	take		5
minutes			
bowl			
table			

Teaching began by matching noun flashcards to actual objects, then focused upon verbs. The words 'the' and 'and' were also introduced at an early stage to permit short phrases to be made from key nouns, eg the table and the cooker.

The success of the introductory block presenting the packet soup recipe confirmed the potential of basic recipe reading, and this was accompanied by a growing realisation that the key nouns and verbs central to the packet soup programme could be readily transferred to form the core of new recipes. Over the following three years the group progressed at an individual rate through a range of over twenty recipes.

a. Extension of project to other senior pupils

Next school session an attempt was made to introduce a new group of four pupils, three of whom had very little previous experience of recognising the written word, to recipe reading. Initial progress was, as expected, slow. However, three did pick up basic noun vocabulary and some key verbs relating to the packet soup programme within the period of a year. Prepositions showed signs of taking longer to master. A fourth pupil, however, whose learning difficulties were further complicated by bi-lingualism, was not ready for the cognitive side of the project, and it was decided to concentrate on her practical skills alone. Interestingly she did continue to make some progress with written vocabulary in later years. As well as promoting a knowledge of key vocabulary and homecraft skills, participation in the project was observed to develop attention and listening skills.

b. Extension to a second special school

When the present author moved to a new post, the recipe reading project was described to staff. The staff felt the project to be relevant in meeting the needs of eight senior pupils. The classteacher to the senior group developed the scheme over the next three years using the following five core recipes:-

    a.   packet soup
    b.   custard
    c.   scrambled egg
    d.   spaghetti hoops
    e.   toasted cheese

In response to the needs of group members, an effort was made to become more weight conscious with an emphasis placed on savoury dishes.

Larger numbers in the project necessitated allocation of time and effort to supporting and supplementing basic programmes using more finely developed organisational techniques, methods and materials. The number of core recipes decreased in direct correspondence to this more intensive approach. The process was greatly facilitated by the growing expertise of staff.

Development of group and individual objectives

As well as long term aims, immediate objectives relating to specific recipes, encompassing new vocabulary, computer linked skills and practical skills were formulated. Individual objectives ensured that each pupil received appropriate challenges at his own level.

Content and structure of sessions

Skills taught at senior level fell into four particular broad areas, a member of staff being required to supervise each of the following activities:-

    a.   introduction of new vocabulary, worksheets, magnetic board etc.
    b.   complete practical cooking task using the recipe reading vocabulary.
    c.   specific additional practice of individual cookery skills eg whisking, use of tin opener etc.
    d.   computer related back-up work.

Sessions were, and continue to be, very staff intensive but by pupil rotation on a variety of activities, attention and interest have increased. The association between cognitive and practical components is emphasised at all stages.

Development of materials

The support materials, teacher manufactured, include

a.   FLASHCARDS (large and small) to support each recipe:
b.   SENTENCE MAKER kits:
c.   DIAGRAMS of ingredients of recipes and actions in sequence:
d.   COMPUTER disks plus overlay sheets and sentence strips.
Writer, CK sequence, CK Match and Flashcards have all been used. An individual Writer disk complete with specific vocabulary has been created to back-up each recipe.
e.   Sets of WORKSHEETS covering a wide range of levels to support
        each recipe.

c. Extension of programme to junior level

As the recipe reading project was being developed at senior level, the programme was being adapted for junior pupils to create a whole school approach. The aim was to introduce pupils to key words at a verbal level prior to formal participation. An integrated theme embracing many areas of the curriculum resulted.

Originally the junior group sessions were structured in a similar manner to those at senior level, this being appropriate to the range of ability within the group at that time. However, with the admission of younger, less able, pupils the following year it became necessary to rethink the structure and content of sessions, addressing lower levels of intellectual functioning and practical ability. A group of seven pupils, four of whom had become confident within the original format and three who were completely new to recipe reading, were involved in the wider development.

The three new pupils were at a very early stage of development and not ready for word recognition, so the emphasis had to be at a pre-formal activity level incorporating extensive work on real object matching, discrimination and naming, moving on to similar activities with photographs and diagrams. Attention span was very short, interest difficult to capture, and each pupil had specific behavioural problems which presented difficulties when aiming for group cohesion.

A short, gentle introduction to recipe reading was required for these pupils before participation in a full session, maintaining a calm working environment. Initially therefore, pupils participated in 10 minutes practical work only on a recipe before progressing to a wider variety of activities as attention control improved and behaviour settled. The focus for the three younger children was on the practical skills while word recognition was incidental; for the older pupils it was important to develop their growing aptitude for word recognition while maximising practical skills potential.

Given the wide range of ability, practical and intellectual, plus behavioural problems present in the group, the recipe chosen had to fulfil the following criteria. The recipe must:

a. provide the opportunity for development in two main areas - practical skills and word recognition:
b. provide the relevant preliminary experiences for expansion at senior level:
c. be within the capabilities, practical and intellectual, of all pupils while placing achievable demands on them:
d. contain familiar vocabulary and use familiar utensils/materials with a very gradual development to incorporate new words:
e. initially be cold, making it safe and appropriate:
f. be interesting enough to stimulate the pupils into participation:
g. offer the opportunity for a high degree of pupil participation making the pupil an active learner:
h. be easily carried out within a classroom.

Areas of the curriculum developed through recipe reading

At junior level the project included work in the following areas of the curriculum: language and communication skills (inclusive of written vocabulary); self help skills; conceptual knowledge, and socialisation and behavioural aspects.

d. Extension to home

Parents of senior pupils had been given regular information about the recipe reading project but insufficient progress had been achieved in generalising recipes of senior pupils to the home situation. A detailed questionnaire was therefore issued to parents concerning the extent of the young adult's present level of involvement in kitchen skills and cooking tasks within the home. Difficulties relating to cooker types and parental anxieties were addressed. Videos were made of each of the six senior pupils carrying out the instructions contained in a scrambled egg recipe. Parents viewed these videos and were also offered the chance to take part in the practical recipe reading task themselves following the same instructions as pupils, concept keyboard computer work, and completing related worksheets. Following these activities, a recipe was selected for each pupil as a target for follow-up work within the home situation. An agenda has therefore been provided for future joint action between home and school.

e. Extension to 16+ establishments

One great advantage of entering the vocabulary of each recipe on the Writer disk is that the content can be easily copied and sent with a pupil on a Leaver's programme to the staff of a further education college, who provided one senior

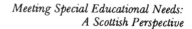

pupil further opportunities to practise the cognitive component of recipe reading work on her once weekly visit to the Unit. It is hoped that similar links can be forged with other centres in the area.

Evaluation

Assessment is ongoing with notes on progress at the end of each session. The project's practical component continues to provide the most relevant assessment information by facilitating checks on pupils' understanding of written material in subsequent practical action. The video recordings have also provided vital assessment information.

The following difficulties have been encountered at both junior and senior level

    a.   time taken to produce materials is extensive;

    b.   home made materials are not sufficiently durable;

    c.   large numbers of staff are required for sessions.

Specific problems experienced at junior level have involved

    a.   difficulties in providing a logical progression of vocabulary, given the constraints placed upon choice of recipe;

    b.   initial pupil distractibility resulting from the range of activities on offer simultaneously;

    c.   length of session.

At senior level difficulties have included

    a.   insufficient opportunity for all pupils to engage more frequently in practical recipe work;

    b.   rote learning of phrases, despite efforts to present vocabulary in different combinations;

    c.   written vocabulary associated with specific recipes is not easily recognised out of context.

Benefits are considered to outweigh heavily any of the disadvantages listed above and include for the juniors

    a.   appropriate and motivating content which has led to improved attention throughout sessions and high levels of pupil participation;

    b.   improved turn taking skills within a concrete meaningful setting;

c.   improved listening skills within group setting;
d.   small gains in basic practical skills;
e.   potential for transferring activities to home setting as a joint focus for parent and child;
f.   improvements in group cohesion and functioning.

Benefits to senior pupils include

a.   growing confidence and pride in achievement;
b.   significantly lengthened attention span in cookery task;
c.   improved safety skills at cooker;
d.   improved manipulation of kitchen utensils;
e.   increased ability to tackle practical task in logical sequence;
f.   enhanced memory of stages of task;
g.   increased naming vocabulary in respect of kitchen equipment;
h.   more purposeful and independent execution of practical skills;
i.   small, key, written vocabulary.

Discussion

Encouraging progress has been apparent in the long term aims of the recipe reading project. As the number of pupils and staff involved has increased, the motivating properties of the scheme have been confirmed.

Most significant gains have been in the development of concentration and attention, drawing independent comment from visitors to the classroom. The recipe reading project has undoubtedly provided a vehicle for the extensive practice of practical kitchen skills, integrating vital factors such as the use of a cooker within a meaningful programme.

Caution must be exercised, however, in making any claims relating to the extent of pupils' written word recognition and vocabulary retention. While pupils have become very proficient in recognising the vocabulary of their current recipe, exposure to vocabulary taken out of context can yield very different results. Nouns have been assimilated most readily along with key verbs whereas recognition of more abstract parts of speech requires the context of an instruction phrase. Pupils' participation in corresponding practical activities has, however, certainly reinforced comprehension of cognitive components. The key to the success of the entire recipe reading project relies upon using the written vocabulary in context and at a concrete level.

Two interesting features were noted during a recent session when individual pupils were presented with a range of flashcards out of context and drawn from a variety of recipes. Word recognition improved quickly when pupils were clued in by being told which recipe the word belonged to and by being given other small pieces of associated information.

As pupils with severe learning difficulties can find it difficult to respond to verbal clues at this sort of general level, a tentative suggestion is that the recipe reading project has strengthened pupils' classification and conceptualisation abilities.

The flexibility factor of the recipe reading project has become apparent over the years. It is further evidenced by the fact that development has been sustained in two schools over a lengthy period, relying entirely on staff innovation to maintain impetus. Both schools have made independent decisions to extend the project to junior level, a further indication of the value placed upon these activities by staff. The project has provided an overall framework covering many areas of the curriculum which pupils can access at their own level. The balance can be tipped in favour of whichever area of development constitutes a priority for the individual pupil.

A final strength of the project lies in the potential for developing really meaningful home - school links with a definite focus, with equal application to both junior and senior pupils. Parental reactions to this idea have been most favourable.

Future developments

Five areas of development have been targetted.

a. The home - school agenda constitutes a priority for the forthcoming term.

b. It is hoped to re-establish links between the two special schools to share information about developments in each establishment, perhaps permitting a more detailed progression of skills to be identified.

c. Now that the junior component of recipe reading is well established, it is intended to take a look at the transition stage between juniors and seniors via a case study of the experience of a particular pupil.

d. A new recipe is currently being prepared for use with the senior group.

e. To maintain impetus guests will be invited into school to share food produced by pupils.

Staff perceive much scope for future development within the project.

References

Reid, J and Low, J (1973). *Link-Up Reading Scheme.* Holmes McDougall Limited.

Mackay, D, Thompson, B and Schaub, P (1970). *Schools Council Programme in Linguistics and English Teaching.* Longman Group Limited.

Trend Series. (1971). Ginn Publishers.

Johnny Black Stories. (1981). Wheaton Publishers.

An Approach to Health Education
for Pupils with
Severe Learning Difficulties

Jo Eales

Introduction

The aim of this chapter is to describe the process of developing a health education programme in a school for pupils with severe learning difficulties, set against the background of current thinking and recommended practice. Particular emphasis is placed on the way in which this health education programme integrated with and influenced the rest of the curriculum, and on the important part which team-teaching contributed to its organisation and delivery. Finally, some conclusions are drawn from these experiences and consideration is given to the implications of teaching health education in special schools.

Background

A clear and useful definition of health education is given in the recently published document 'Promoting Good Health' (SHEG/SCCC, 1990).

> Health education is concerned with quality of life and with the promotion of the physical, social and mental well-being of the individual. It involves not only imparting knowledge about what is beneficial and what is harmful but it also involves the development of skills which will help individuals to use their knowledge effectively.

In recent years health education has achieved a higher profile in schools in response, amongst other things, to increased public awareness and concern over such things as alcohol and drug misuse and currently, the emergence of HIV/AIDS and the high reported incidence of the physical and sexual abuse of children. This has prompted a reappraisal of the way in which health education is taught in schools. There has been a move away from the traditional idea of health education being about personal hygiene and 'the facts of life' with problematic issues being broached in an *ad hoc* fashion as and when they arose. Instead a coherent, planned and co-ordinated health education programme is advocated, which emphasises the positive aspects of healthy lifestyles. It is seen as essentially pupil-centred with the central theme of enhancing and developing pupils' self-esteem to enable them to take more responsibility for their own health and well-being. This is to be achieved by acquiring knowledge and information, developing increased awareness of themselves and others, and being conscious of the consequences of their own actions in order to take informed decisions over health choices.

Health education is seen as a continuing and progressive process, 'the spiral approach', lasting throughout a child's time in school. Appropriate learning opportunities can then be introduced to coincide with different ages and stages of development. These can appear in the curriculum in different ways, either as a distinct element with its own time or as an essential element integrated with other subjects or by using teaching opportunities as they occur. Often a combination of these approaches will be used. In addition, health education is seen as permeating the informal or 'hidden' curriculum of relationships within the school and with the wider community. It is, therefore, necessary for schools to define and state the values, attitudes and beliefs upon which they operate. A 'whole school' policy on health education can then be used to achieve congruence between its stated aims and practices.

Fundamental to all these recommendations is the recognition that health education is a joint responsibility which schools share with parents. It is therefore seen as essential that schools keep parents informed about the programme and involve them as closely as possible.

It is not, however, easy to meet these ideal criteria as a recent quote from the Director General of the World Health Organisation indicates:

> Despite convincing proof of their effectiveness, why are there still so few strong health education curricula in schools? (SHEG/WHO, 1989)

One of the reasons is, undoubtedly, the complex nature of the subject and the sensitive moral and ethical issues which it raises. For this reason, teachers often feel that they lack the necessary competence and/or confidence to tackle it. There is a recognition in both special and mainstream education of the need to teach health and sex education. A survey conducted in Scotland amongst schools for pupils with severe learning difficulties indicated, however, that whilst half had established a policy and programme for health and sex education, the other half saw it as a priority but a problematic area for development (Watson *et al.* 1989).

The development of the Westfield health and sex education programme

These doubts and uncertainties were also experienced by the teaching staff at Westfield School, a small school of about forty pupils with severe and very severe learning difficulties ranging from age five to sixteen years and over. At the beginning of the 1986-1987 session there was some internal reorganisation which led to the creation of a 'senior school' rather than senior classes as had previously existed. This coincided with the author's appointment as Assistant Head Teacher with the remit of organising the senior school and reviewing its curriculum.

Senior School was arranged in three class groups with approximately six to eight pupils in each of the age bands 11 to 14 years, 14 to 16 years and 16 years and over, respectively. Each class was staffed by a teacher, assisted by a nursery nurse. All pupils were physically mobile and had some speech but most had communication difficulties. Cognitive ability varied greatly, as did physical, social and emotional maturity.

Origins of the programme

When we examined the existing curriculum we found a significant gap in that it took no account of the pupils' sexuality. We were, therefore, trying to prepare them for the transition to adulthood in terms of the acquisition of independence skills, whilst ignoring the fundamental physical, social and emotional changes which all teenagers experience at adolescence. It was at this stage that we decided to embark on a health and sex education programme and over the succeeding weeks the staff involved discussed their own feelings about it and the rationale which would influence and shape its aims, approaches, content and methods. Ann Craft's book (1987) provided a useful starting point for these discussions. In the book, she refers to Hilary Brown's statement that 'many handicapped young people face the emotional and physical changes of adolescence amidst a conspiracy of silence from those of us 'in the know'.' We agreed with this statement and felt that our pupils could easily be both frightened and vulnerable if these changes and their implications were not explained to them. We also felt that their vulnerability was compounded by communication difficulties, lack of assertiveness and, often, low self-esteem.

We also felt strongly about the importance of involving parents. This is also considered in Ann Craft's book, where it is pointed out that adolescence can be a very stressful time for parents when they realise that their child is becoming an adult with all that this implies for the future. We wanted to acknowledge to both ourselves and parents that health education was a shared responsibility between home and school. We did not see ourselves as 'experts' in this area and wanted to know parents' views and concerns from the programme's inception rather than presenting it to them as a *fait accompli*.

Planning the programme

Meetings were arranged with parents and proved informative, honest and frank. Identifying particular issues and concerns helped greatly in organising teaching groups and choosing appropriate resources. A more detailed description of our parental liaison is contained in Craft and Cromby (1991). After several meetings with parents the staff were able to define the aims for the programme which were:

a.   To enable pupils to learn how they grow and develop, emphasising the physical and emotional changes which occur at adolescence and how to cope with them.

b.   To make pupils more aware of the socially acceptable forms of behaviour expected of adults, including the constraints of sexual behaviour.

c.   To help pupils to get on with others and to know how to behave in different situations.

d.   To enable pupils to express their feelings in a confident, appropriate and acceptable way and to appreciate the effect of their behaviour on others and vice-versa.

e.   To encourage pupils to make choices and take decisions about their everyday lives and to accept responsibility for their personal needs and safety.

The programme and the curriculum

Having established our long-term teaching aims, we were then able to consider the curriculum framework, approaches and content of the programme and its links with other curricular areas. Important features of our approach to the programme were that:

a.   We chose to call it 'Growing Up' to reflect our view that health education should be broadly based, containing elements of physical, social and emotional development and that sex education, whilst important, should not be the major focus of interest.

b.   It would be progressive in nature, lasting throughout pupils' time in senior school.

c.   It would take into account their age and stage of development.

d.   A 'spiral model' would be adopted, in that topics could be re-visited and covered at greater depth where appropriate.

e.   Learning would be mainly experiential and activity-based using methods such as those suggested in 'Not a Child Anymore' (Brook Advisory Centres, 1987): i.e. guided discussions; drawing on pupils' own experiences; using trigger materials such as TV programmes, videos, slides, pictures and stories; drama and role-play; games and trust exercises and individual counselling.

We also decided to use 'private' as a pivotal concept to emphasise individuals' rights to their own body, possessions and places. This could then be used when going on to talk about appropriate behaviour and 'good' and 'bad' touching. The two broad areas which we used as the framework for the curriculum were those of growth and development and relationships.

The topic chosen as our starting point was 'myself'. As well as providing a logical beginning we felt that it was non-threatening and would create an atmosphere of trust and confidence. It was also a means of building on pupils' existing knowledge and experience whilst incorporating work on self-image and self-awareness. There was then a natural progression to looking at 'myself and others'; stages of development from birth to adulthood; emotional and physical changes at adolescence; sexual intercourse and conception and the birth process and parenthood.

The area of relationships, including feelings, responsibilities, appropriate behaviour and safety, was covered using any activities formal or informal which provided natural learning opportunities. 'Relationships' was also the prime focus for drama and began by getting pupils used to working together in groups to create a story or play which involved choosing a theme and deciding on how the plot would unfold. Having established co-operative and group work skills it was then possible to use role-play and games to practise self-assertiveness, appropriate behaviour and to explore and express emotions.

In the first year of the 'Growing Up' programme we also provided specific and related teaching on self-help skills and language. Self-help skills highlighted the importance of healthy eating and aspects of personal presentation and hygiene. Language sessions dealt with describing personal appearance, preferences and interests and being able to communicate important personal details. They were also used to enable pupils to acquire the vocabulary and language associated with body parts and functions.

In the second year we introduced some environmental studies with topics on water, electricity and colours to complement teaching on safety.

The success of team-teaching in health education encouraged us to extend this approach to physical education and music. This enabled staff to link both the aims and curriculum content of health education to these areas, both of which had great potential for developing pupils' self confidence and self-awareness. As the health education programme developed we were able to see how well it fitted into the rest of the curriculum and this encouraged us to provide new experiences such as outdoor education activities, yoga and the production of an annual pantomime to increase pupils' sense of personal achievement.

The following diagram illustrates how aspects of the 'Growing Up' programme permeated through the whole curriculum.

Links between health education and other curricular elements

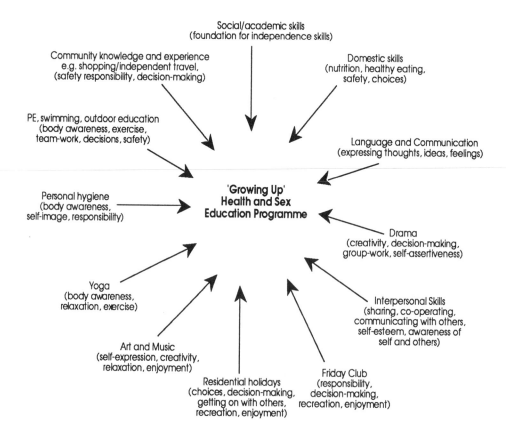

The organisation of the programme based on team-teaching

We had decided early on in our school re-organisation to use some team-teaching in the senior school. This would enable us to maximise staff resources, make better use of the available classroom space and give pupils the opportunity to experience different teaching personalities and styles in a similar way to their peers in mainstream education. The 'Growing Up' health education programme seemed an ideal place to begin team-teaching in that it was a new venture which would require much discussion and mutual support. We also believed that, given the sensitive nature of some of the content, it would be more acceptable to have a range of views represented, out of which a broad consensus could be reached.

As Assistant Head Teacher, with responsibility for the senior school, I had non-contact time available during the week for curriculum development and therefore took on the role of co-ordinator of the programme. In the initial stages this involved arranging the parents' meetings and guiding discussions about the basic framework of the programme with staff. I also had the time to research appropriate resources and, as was often the case, to modify them for our own use. Once the programme was under way, my role included time-tabling, evaluation, and forward planning.

To begin with, team meetings were held after school, but once the programme began we used our professional preparation time within the school day, which enabled nursery nurses to participate. One hour per week was allocated to a teaching session involving all pupils and staff which was co-led, i.e. a topic was chosen and then responsibility for leading the sessions was shared. Each teacher took a short series of sessions and developed it in her own way. Follow-up work on a class basis was also provided by that member of staff. In addition, each teacher, assisted by a nursery nurse, took another one and a half hour slot during the week when pupils were divided into three mixed groups and rotated for related subjects as described previously. Teachers used their own preparation time to plan their sessions of work, details of which were circulated to the team in the form of lesson outlines for the term.

Although most of the sessions were presented by teachers, we were able to include other people with particular skills and expertise. The school nurse gave some extremely enjoyable and popular presentations on basic first aid procedures and what to expect from a visit to the doctor or hospital. These were expertly done and involved lots of practical work and role play. The local community police team became regular visitors to the school, providing input on road safety and cycling proficiency as well as running discos at the pupils' Friday Club. A parent who was a member of the local fire-service came to talk to us about his experiences, and to demonstrate equipment as well as arranging for a fire-engine to visit the school. We also received two terms of yoga lessons given by a local teacher and a youth strategy worker came to do small-group work with some of the pupils. Team-

c

teaching facilitated these contributions by providing sufficient staff resources for adequate briefing and support for visitors and time to give and receive necessary feedback. It also provided a valuable way of evaluating the programme in that when not directly involved in teaching, staff could observe and evaluate pupils' reactions and modify it accordingly.

Conclusions

The health education programme is continuing at Westfield School. Staff have gained knowledge and expertise over the years helped by an increasingly wide range of teaching resources, most of which can be obtained through the Lothian Area Health Education Resource Centre in Edinburgh. Further details of useful resources are listed in Watson, Mackay and Eales (1989).

Our approach at Westfield School was eclectic, drawing from a large number of health education sources. To some extent we learned by trial and error but on reflection this was a valuable experience in the long term. It was reassuring to discover subsequently that many of the ideas which we arrived at independently were in fact considered good practice by others in the field.

The concepts which we found most useful in structuring our programme were those of the spiral model relating teaching to ages and stages of development, the adoption of a simple but flexible framework capable of incorporating change and a planned and co-ordinated approach based on team-teaching.

Although it is possible for schools to devise their own programmes as we did, it would be very helpful to have a curriculum framework and guidelines when setting up a health education programme for use with pupils who have learning difficulties. This would establish basic principles and some guidance on appropriate teaching methods and resources.

Local regional guidelines have been produced for mainstream primary and secondary schools, but they include little information about specific approaches which could be used, for example, for pupils with severe or profound learning difficulties or physical and sensory impairments.

The advantages of teaching health education in our particular setting have been demonstrated in the following ways:

> Pupils have shown little embarrassment about the sex education content of the course. Rather, they have taken pride in their knowledge and see it as a symbol of adult status. Many subjects not previously raised by pupils, which were perhaps thought of as 'taboo' are now openly discussed (eg. bodily functions; feelings). For this to have happened we feel that we have created an atmosphere of trust and safety. We are now able to talk to parents more openly about a wide variety of issues and concerns because of the existence of the

programme. We are very much more aware of the need to provide opportunities and experiences across the curriculum to develop pupils' self-esteem and autonomy.

The only disadvantage that we have found in teaching health education is that there are no easy answers in an area that requires a great deal of sensitivity to pupils' individual needs. Staff regret that, in common with many special schools, we have no male members of staff to provide male role models in a school population with a preponderance of boys.

We are aware of shortfalls and gaps in our programme when compared with recent recommendations which include the community and environmental dimension of health education as a major foundation stone of the programme with 'growth and development' and 'relationships'. Hopefully, the forthcoming Scottish Office Education Department guidelines on 'Curriculum and Assessment 5-14' in Environmental Studies and Cross Curricular Aspects and Issues will be helpful in this respect.

Finally we recognise the need to introduce a pattern of planned and coherent health education for younger pupils including parental involvement.

Implications of teaching health education in special schools

There is often a tendency to emphasise the difficulties of teaching health education to pupils with special needs. Although these are real and cannot be ignored, on the basis of our experience with the 'Growing Up' programme at Westfield, there would also seem to be many positive aspects. Special schools are usually smaller and have a higher staff-pupil ratio than those in mainstream. This can facilitate the planning and co-ordination of health education and with the creation of senior teacher posts it could well be possible to give such a person the role of health education co-ordinator.

The focus in special schools has traditionally been pupil-centred, aimed at assessing and meeting individual needs in a holistic way and using teaching methods based on practical experience and activities. All of these approaches are now being recommended as good practice in health education.

Staff in special schools also tend to be in close and regular contact with parents and already acknowledge the idea of parents as co-educators. There is, therefore, already a good basis for liaison and involvement between staff and parents over health education.

Many special schools have pupils from the age of five up to sixteen plus, giving them an excellent opportunity to develop a cohesive health education programme which can span the pupil's school career without a transitional break between primary and secondary stages.

Particularly in schools for children with severe and profound learning difficulties, there is not the same pressure to meet national testing or examination criteria. The curriculum may then be sufficiently flexible to enable health education to be promoted as a discrete, integrated and permeating element within it.

Finally, health education has always played an important role in the curriculum of pupils with learning difficulties though its focus may have been narrow. The so-called 'hidden' curriculum in mainstream schools often forms a major part of the explicit and formal curriculum in special education where teaching social and interpersonal skills is of the utmost importance when they cannot be learned incidentally.

The combination of these traditions, experiences and expertise in the special sector, allied with the growing availability of appropriate teaching resources can give special schools a distinct advantage when embarking on a planned and co-ordinated health education programme.

References

Brook Advisory Centres (1987). *Not a Child Anymore - A Complete Social and Sex Education Programme for Young Adults with a Mental Handicap.* Brook Advisory Centres Education and Publications Unit.

Craft, A (1987). *Mental Handicap and Sexuality, Issues and Perspectives.* Costello.

Craft, A and Cromby, J (1991). *Parental Involvement in the Sex Education of Students with Severe Learning Difficulties.* Department of Mental Handicap, University of Nottingham Medical School.

Scottish Health Education Group/Scottish Consultative Council on the Curriculum (1990). *Promoting Good Health: Proposals for Action in Schools.* Scottish Health Education Group.

Scottish Health Education Group/World Health Organisation Report (1989). *The Healthy School.*

Watson, J, Mackay, M and Eales, J (1989). *Autonomy and the Curriculum for Pupils with Severe Learning Difficulties: A Report of Two Developments.* Moray House College, Edinburgh.

Developing Communication and Language Skills in Pre-School Children with Down's Syndrome.

Elizabeth C Dean and Jane Davidson

Introduction

Within the speech therapy profession in recent years there has been a realisation that to provide effective treatment the clinician must take account not only of the aims set for the client but also of the way in which these will be achieved; that there should be more emphasis on how the client 'learns' in therapy. Due primarily to advances in linguistic and psychological theory, speech and language therapists have become increasingly skilled in making an accurate diagnosis of the level at which the communication process breaks down. Having completed detailed assessments the therapist is in the ideal position to determine the aims for a particular client. These may emphasise preverbal, verbal, augmentative (for example, speech and sign) or alternative communication skills. However, it is sometimes more difficult, within the constraints of the therapy session, to decide how to organise the learning experience for individual children. The literature on speech therapy with children with Down's Syndrome illustrates this point (Thurman, 1989). Whilst there are many pointers about the features which should be incorporated in speech therapy programmes, for example, the value of early intervention, close collaboration with parents, the use of everyday routines as a focus for therapy, and the combination of verbal and non-verbal means of communication, these features are concerned in the main with the aim of therapy and not with the way in which the remedial situation should be organised to maximise learning potential. This chapter describes a project designed to explore how the therapeutic situation might be ordered so that the child with Down's Syndrome can most easily learn language.

The project was funded by the Edinburgh branch of the Scottish Down's Syndrome Association, to allow the authors to devise a speech therapy programme and evaluate its effectiveness. Initially eight children were involved, of whom seven completed the project. Efficacy was evaluated against the bench mark of data published in 1985 by Cunningham, Glenn, Wilkinson & Sloper. In a study of young children with Down's Syndrome who were involved in an early intervention programme which did not involve specific speech therapy, Cunningham *et al.* found that language skills developed more slowly than cognition (as measured in symbolic play) and that the lag increased with age and was more apparent for boys than girls. Their findings allowed a comparison to be made which indicated that the specific speech therapy programme used in the Queen Margaret College study did have a positive effect on the communicative and linguistic skills of pre-school children with Down's Syndrome.

As the therapeutic programme is the focus of the paper we will describe the rationale on which remediation was based first. Then we will consider in more detail how therapy was organised for individual children.

The therapy programme: rationale

The importance of a language environment which is rich and where communication occurs contingent on the child's response is often stressed for children with normally developing speech and language. However, such a setting can be difficult to 'manufacture' in the clinic and, indeed, many of the children referred to speech therapy have experienced such a language environment within the home. These children, due to their linguistic or learning difficulties, require more structured experiences to allow them to abstract information about language and to interact communicatively.

How can we manipulate the clinic setting to provide such situations? An approach which may provide some clues is the current research on event knowledge which has led to the formulation of Event Theory (Nelson, 1986).

> Nelson and her colleagues suggest that young children organise their understanding of common experiences in terms of a general event representation (GER). Experiences are understood in terms of specific contexts, the roles adopted by people within those contexts and the actions performed by the children themselves. Frequently occurring activities which have a specific purpose, clearly defined roles for the participants and a set of materials or props which are regularly employed, may become particularly well established in the child's mind. The mental representations of such events are referred to as scripts. (Harris, 1988)

Scripting is an early process in the representation of experience and Constable in Nelson (1986) describes scripts as the basic units of analysis within the cognitive system.

The ability to find, recognise, select and organise the mass of stimuli available to the child is vital if patterns are to be recognised so that cognitive and linguistic development can continue through this process of reorganisation and assimilation. In Event Theory scripts are seen as arising from experience and as forming the basis of future processing.

> ...... the greater the extent to which an event in context is 'scripted'

the more easily it appears to be assimilated for the formation of a generalised event representation - a "basic building block" for further cognitive (and perhaps linguistic) analyses. (Constable, 1986)

Other authors have worked upon similar lines. Bruner (1983) described mothers and children creating predictable formats of interaction which act as microcosms for communication and for establishing a shared reality. Bruner argues that the transactions that occur in such formats constitute the 'input' from which children master grammar, how to refer and mean, and how to realise intentions communicatively.

The obvious question is, how can we use these formats/routines/events to enhance language development? Constable argues that the relevance of Event Theory is that it provides a framework for the way in which the nonlinguistic features of the therapeutic situation can be ordered to ensure the creation of an optimum situation for language learning.

Event Theory stresses that events are predictable - that is that they have a highly specified temporal form, one example being a form in which component acts mean that the use of particular objects, actions and interactions are repeated several times. The research suggests that the more scripted an event is, i.e. the more predictable its form, the more efficiently it can be processed. If external events are well linked to the child's script (its mental representation of the event) the script may guide the child automatically through the event. This gives the child 'cognitive space'; free processing capacity which allows him to consider the problematic aspects of the situation - in this case language.

So scripted events can reduce the cognitive workload and therefore increase the resources the child can apply to language learning. Scripted events facilitate display of the child's more advanced communicative and linguistic performance.

Bruner (1983) states that much of early infant interaction takes place in constrained, familiar situations and shows a surprising degree of order and 'systematicity'. He supports this by arguing that children spend long periods engaged in a very limited range of activities and within each of these restricted 'domains' there is a striking systematicity. He gives the example of a simple act like hammering which is applied successively to a wide range of objects over quite lengthy periods. Bruner further argues that the acquisition of prelinguistic and linguistic communication takes place, in the main, in highly constrained settings. In these the child and the caregiver combine elements in the situations to extract meanings, assign interpretations, and infer intentions.

Evidence of children's pleasure and interest in routine situations or scripted events also comes from clinical experience. Ask a mother to play with her child and within the constraints of the clinic situation she will probably choose to engage in a number of familiar routines; perhaps, for a young child, turn taking games, songs or naming games.

Many parents build a routine around the story reading situation. The child is encouraged to participate by means of a strategy termed 'scaffolding' - the process by which the adult provides the general structure of the conversation and leaves the child to fill in gaps chosen because they match the child's linguistic ability. Typically, when reading stories, parents begin by reading the whole story until the child becomes familiar with it. At this point the caregiver begins to omit part of the storyline on a page - often the last word i.e. "And Daddy Bear said 'Who's been sleeping on my ....?' ". The contribution asked of the child will be extended as the child's linguistic development allows more sophisticated contribution.

Bruner and Nelson argue that for children to make sense of their world they need to be involved in routines which have a clear structure and which facilitate communicative interactions. If this is true for children who are learning normally, it has even greater implications for those with learning disorders.

Harris suggests that these theoretical notions can be translated into specific strategies for encouraging language development. These strategies would differ from traditional approaches because speech and language would apparently not be the central focus - language would not be 'taught' even in an indirect way. Instead the child would be involved in activities which are structured to provide the optimum conditions for the development of communication.

The routines chosen are structured in order that the cognitive processing required by the child is minimised so that all possible processing capacity is available for language. This is in marked contrast with language learning approaches which continually involve the child in stimulating and challenging situations. These rich and complex settings utilised commonly in therapy are obviously essential for cognitive development to take place and are an integral part of normal language development in children who can learn from only a brief exposure to linguistic information. However, as we have discussed, children with learning disorders may require a different approach to language learning. For them the individual levels of language (for example, the ability to convey meaning, the ability to combine words into a sentence and the ability to combine sounds into words) and communication need to be made tangible and accessible. This has been demonstrated to be valuable for other groups of children with linguistic difficulties. Dean & Howell have utilised metalinguistic awareness successfully in the treatment of children with developmental sound system disorders, (Dean & Howell, 1986; Dean, Howell, Hill & Waters, 1990; Howell & Dean, 1987, 1991). The specific routines we describe in this chapter allow children to abstract relevant knowledge about speech, language and communication by maximising the attention they can devote to the linguistic aspects of the situation.

Within an Event Theory framework the activity remains substantially the same with linguistic demands being increased as the child progresses. This is in marked contrast to common therapeutic approaches in which the activity itself is often made more complex as the child succeeds in meeting the demands of the situation.

Working within the potentially artificial setting of the clinic it seemed important to begin with routines which come from everyday life and which are already well known to the child. This helps the clinician to achieve the first aim of making the routine familiar and predictable. In addition, utilising real life events will allow the learning to be generalised to settings outside the clinic. This may happen in two ways - firstly the insights gained by the child in the clinic situation will have the opportunity of being reinforced regularly at home, and secondly, the insights parents hopefully gain (from being involved in each session) into the way in which linguistic processing can be maximised can be applied to similar situations which arise naturally at home. Thus for both the parent and child the language learning that takes place in speech therapy is closely linked with the communication that takes place at home.

Having considered the theoretical rationale on which the therapy programme was based, we will now describe how these ideas were put into practice for a group of pre-school children with Down's Syndrome.

The therapy programme: assessment

Initially the children were assessed using the same assessments employed by Cunningham *et al.* (1985) to allow comparison of the results.

Assessment	Aim
Reynell Developmental Language Scales (Revised) (Reynell, 1977)	To measure understanding of spoken language.
Symbolic Play Test (Lowe and Costello, 1979)	To provide an indication of symbolic functioning and therefore of general cognitive level (see Cunningham *et al.* 1985).

In addition, several assessments were used to gain a more complete picture of each individual child's performance. These included assessments of communicative functioning (Dewart & Summers 1988), Revised Edinburgh Functional Communication Profile (Wirz, Skinner & Dean, 1990) and a recorded sample of expressive language. None of the children in the study was able to co-operate in testing on the Reynell Developmental Language Scale (RDLS) Expressive Scale; however several produced some output in speech and/or sign. To try to represent this in a comparable form the output of each child was then converted to an age equivalent score using the first section of the RDLS Expressive Language Scale. Whilst it is recognised that this is a rather crude measure it did allow profiling of the children's expressive language performance which would have been masked by formal RDLS Expressive Language Scale scoring.

An interview with the parents was also carried out to allow their views of the child's strengths and needs to be incorporated into the programme. During each session the child's output (spoken and signed) was recorded and halfway through the project parents were asked their views of the work and of their child's progress. After the final therapy session all the assessments were repeated.

The therapy programme

The intervention process described in this chapter is perhaps best seen as consisting of two layers, both of which require to be based on a theoretical rationale; to be assessed (to determine the aims and structure of the programme); and to be evaluated.

There is first the layer at which the speech, language and/or communication disorder has to be assessed and profiled with aims being constructed for the child's future development. There is then the layer within which the optimum language learning situation for each child is identified and a plan constructed as to the way in which these conditions can be provided. Let us consider these two layers separately.

The therapy programme: communication aims

The initial assessment sessions enabled the formation of a linguistic profile for each child. This took account not only of the results of formal tests and analysis, but also of the views of the parents, expressed during interviews.

For each child a potential 'route' for communicative development was drawn up as a guideline to the speech, language or communication behaviours therapy would aim to encourage. The interaction might take place through speech, or through speech and sign, and the hierarchy provided a guide to the language structures that might most profitably give a model for the child's own communication attempts.

To clarify this level of the intervention process it is possible to give examples of hypothetical aims. Depending on the developmental level the linguistic aims might be concerned primarily with encouraging the essential, nonverbal prerequisites for communication.

One such set of aims might read:

Language aims (preverbal)
1.   To encourage turn taking (to help the child to learn that a basic feature of communication is that the speaker and listener take turns).
2.   To encourage 'requesting' behaviour (to show the child that if he can indicate a need nonverbally, ie by stretching out a hand to be lifted up, he can indicate his wants).

As the child's communicative abilities develop the aims will change, for example:

Language aims (vocal)
1.   To encourage the child to 'request' action by making a sound.
2.   To encourage the child to 'request' an object by making a sound.

Later the target will be verbal or signed, for example:
1.   To encourage use of individual words after cueing.
2.   To encourage spontaneous use of individual words.

More advanced aims might include:
3.   To encourage the expression of possession ie dolly's head.
4.   To encourage the expression of position ie **on** the table **under** the chair.

Whilst these aims are organised in a loose hierarchy, in that communicative behaviours the child would usually acquire earliest are at the top of the list, this progression is not rigid as it would not be in normal development. All the stated aims for each child may be the focus of attention at specific points during the therapy programme.

In addition, for each child, a list was compiled of the signs currently used and those to be taught. Thus any of the aims could be achieved by the child speaking or signing or using a combination of speech and sign and the clinician's input was altered accordingly.

The therapy programme : the language learning situation
The earlier sections of this chapter set out the theoretical rationale, based on Event Theory, which this study adopted. The routines were chosen to be motivating for each child and the help of parents and caregivers was invaluable in achieving this. The actual routines used depended on many factors; the child's interests, mobility and the communication or linguistic aims to be encouraged.

Examples of the routines used with the seven children studied in this project can be grouped into three categories reflecting the aims of the intervention process. These routines were designed to encourage communicative behaviours, linguistic skills, and to build the foundations of spoken language development by focusing on phonological awareness.

Before giving specific examples of these routines, it will perhaps be useful to give a practical illustration of how the assessment and planning stages can be organised. Although several of the stages could be said to be self-evident, we have included them for the sake of completeness and because this process may be unfamiliar to some readers.

The therapy planning process

1. Build a relationship with the child.
2. Carry out a comprehensive linguistic assessment, covering ie, interaction, understanding and use of language, and the speech sound system (as appropriate).
3. Specify the linguistic factors which will determine the verbal input to the child and will influence the choice of routine.
4. In consultation with the caregiver choose a few (eg 3) routines to try.
5. Introduce the routines to the child to decide whether they prove motivating and interesting.
6. Plan how the linguistic aims and routines can be assimilated.
7. Begin therapy with the child.
8. Re-assess the aims and choice of routine in the light of the child's response.

See Appendix 1 for a practical application of this planning process.

What routines have proved useful during the study? We can divide them into groups according to the aim for which we have employed them.

Communication routines

Joint action routines; games in which turntaking is encouraged, eg ball games; cause and effect games where action is contingent upon communication from the child, eg letting a car go down a slope when the child signs or vocalises in a consistent form.

Language routines in which both comprehension and output can be facilitated

setting the table
feeding the dolly
bathing the dolly

    dressing the dolly
    setting out animals in a farm
    washing clothes
    washing dishes
    putting furniture/people into a doll's house
    drawing parts of a man on the board
    book routines.

Comprehension can be the focus of the activity if the clinician structures her input so that the child is having to 'decode' or understand sentence structures and vocabulary which are at the limit of processing ability. Examples of progressively more complex structures which could be incorporated in a doll's house game include:- "Put the doll in the house". "Put the doll and the chair in the house". "Put the doll in the house and the chair in the box". This is a similar progression to that used in the Derbyshire Language Scheme (Knowles & Masidlover, 1982).

The child's use of spoken language or sign can be facilitated by means of several strategies, for example, forced choice questions. The input of the clinician to a child setting the table might be:-

    Let's set the table.
    What do we need?
    Do you want a cup or a plate?
    A plate, that's it, a plate for dolly.
    Now ... do you want a fork or a cup?
    A fork. Do you need a spoon too?   Here it is.
    Who will sit here, mummy or teddy?
    Oh it's teddy's place.   Sit down teddy.
    Is teddy hungry or thirsty?
    I see. He wants a drink.
    That's better teddy.
    Now - do you want a big cup or a small cup?
    A big one ... of course.
    Are you having milk or juice?
    Juice ... can I have juice too?

The clinician may use 'scaffolding' when the child has to fill in progressively more of an utterance, or take increasing responsibility for the verbal interaction. For instance when bathing dolly the adult may initially use the following language:-

    Look at dolly - she is dirty.
    What shall we do?   Bath her!

What do we need?
Here's the bath.
Let's fill it with water.
What else do we need?
A bar of soap.
Shall we wash dolly?
Scrub a dub dub a doll in a tub.
I'm washing her leg.
Now dolly's all clean.

This could be altered gradually to allow the child to contribute:-

Look at dolly she is ....
What shall we do?......................
What do we need?
Here's the ....
Let's fill it with........................
What else do we need?
A bar of.................................
Shall we wash dolly?
Scrub a .... a doll in a ....
I'm washing her arm.
You're washing her.....................
Now dolly is all........................

To exemplify these points the language of the clinician has been reduced to an extent which sounds rather false.   However they illustrate the way in which strategies such as 'scaffolding' and forced choice questions can encourage vocalisation within familiar routines.   It is the fact that the routine is well known to the child and predictable that allows the child to contribute to the interaction at the earliest possible stage.   Later he will transfer these linguistic skills to novel situations.   Within therapy the initial set of routines chosen for each child can be utilised for up to six sessions, or even more, the complexity of the language being extended as the child's communication skills develop.   So a routine which initially stimulated comprehension of language may then be extended linguistically to facilitate output.   With all routines the clinician's input may be spoken, or combined with sign as appropriate.   Similarly we have accepted spoken or signed output by the child as being equally valid.

Speech sound awareness routines

The final set of routines we will discuss are rather different in that, for the authors, they represented a diversion from normal therapeutic practice. The author's initial impetus with these pre-school Down's Syndrome children had been the development of language skills. Within speech therapy it has traditionally been accepted that the first focus should be the child's ability to convey meaning and that work on speech sound production should follow at a later date. However, parents often see a degree of clarity of speech as being vital if their child's attempts at spoken language are to be recognised and understood. Indeed parents in the study pointed to their children's obvious attempts to move their utterance closer to the target utterance. They, like normally developing children, showed an awareness of the properties of the speech sound system; specifically an awareness that their speech was not close enough to the target utterance to be understood and subsequent attempts to repair the utterance to make it more intelligible. The importance of such metalinguistic awareness in the development of the speech sound system has been an interest within the speech therapy clinic at Queen Margaret College, where its role in the remediation of speech sound disorders has been studied. (Dean & Howell, 1986; Dean, Howell, Hill & Waters, 1990; Howell & Dean, 1987, 1991).

To take account of the parents' concerns about the development of intelligible speech, and to try to support individual children's attempts to make themselves understood, we devised a set of routines aimed at increasing the children's awareness of the properties of sounds and encouraging them to play with sounds in order to develop an awareness that sounds can be manipulated. These routines were only used with children whose attempts to repair utterances indicated that they currently had the potential to develop such an awareness.

Examples of routines used:-

Routines to emphasise rhyming
Nursery rhymes and action sounds.

Routines to emphasise rhythm
Clapping games and songs.

Routines to develop sound awareness
Focusing the child's attention on the sound formation of words, e.g. playing with a box of toys whose names all begin with the same phoneme. The child's attention was drawn to this phoneme in isolation (in the clinician's speech) and in words but at no stage was the child required to produce the word unless he did so spontaneously. The aim was merely to raise the child's awareness of phonemes in isolation and in context.

Routines to develop sound play
Babbling games using, e.g. mirrors, puppets, tape recorders, bubbles.

Having introduced these routines in a rather tentative way it rapidly became apparent that the children working with them were interested in and motivated by these activities indicating that they were a very positive addition to the therapy programme.

Measuring efficacy
Having a specific rationale for facilitating communication and language skills meant that it was possible to study the effect this therapy programme had on the seven pre-school Down's Syndrome children in the study. See Table 1.

Table 1: Subject Details

Subject	Age at beginning of project	Sex
1	1.07	F
2	2.04	M
3	2.05	F
4	3.01	M
5	3.02	F
6	3.08	M
7	4.02	M

The children had one session of speech therapy each fortnight (an average of nine therapy sessions and four assessment sessions over six months). Parents were always encouraged to be present. Watching the work gave a practical illustration of the suggestions later made for continuing the programme at home.

As previously discussed, each child's language skills were assessed using the Reynell Developmental Language Scales (Revised) (Reynell, 1977), and symbolic functioning was assessed using the Symbolic Play Test (Lowe & Costello, 1976). Using these assessments age equivalent scores for expressive and receptive language processing and symbolic functioning could be estimated. Our hope was that speech therapy would reduce the lag of language behind symbolic functioning that Cunningham *et al.* (1985) had demonstrated for children with Down's Syndrome.

Results

Figures A - G detail age equivalencies calculated from subjects' scores on each of the assessments. The data are presented in graph form to allow comparison of each child's pre- and post-therapy performance in each of the assessed areas.

The first question we asked was how many of the subjects initially demonstrated an age equivalency on the Symbolic Play Test in advance of their age equivalencies calculated from the RDLS. Study of Figures A and B shows that only two of the children demonstrated this pattern, Subjects 3 and 5. What changes occurred in these children's performance after therapy? Subject 3's age equivalent scores indicated that the lag of language behind cognition had been reduced to almost nothing for expressive language and had been not only eliminated but 'reversed' so that the age equivalent score for comprehension was in advance of that for symbolic functioning. Subject 5 had rather different results with expressive language performance improving but remaining behind symbolic play age equivalencies; comprehension age equivalencies remained static.

So, what was the pattern of change in the children who did not initially demonstrate Symbolic Play Test scores in advance of language scores? Subject 2 (Figure C) and Subject 4 (see Figure D) initially appeared to be functioning at similar levels for symbolic play and language, although Subject 4 had slightly higher comprehension of language scores. For both these children, post-therapy, language scores had risen leaving Symbolic Play Test Scores relatively static.

Subject 6 (see Figure E) presented, pre-therapy, with roughly equivalent Symbolic Play Test and RDLS comprehension scores but with a rather lower expressive language age equivalency. Post-therapy his performance on the latter assessment had improved slightly but otherwise performance was relatively static. Subject 7 (Figure F) proved very difficult to assess initially and pre-therapy age equivalencies were probably rather lower than would have been expected. However, post-therapy the age equivalencies could all be calculated (an improvement in itself) and were roughly equivalent for all three assessments. Graphs such as that provided in Figure F are liable to misrepresent the actuality because the initial assessment scores are probably not representative of Subject 7's performance and it would be misleading to claim that all the improvement indicated in Figure F actually took place within the period of study. However, the figure gives an indication of Subject 7's ability to co-operate in testing pre- and post-therapy and of final performance levels.

Subject 1 (Figure G) presents rather a different picture. Initially age equivalencies for all three assessments appeared similar, primarily because Subject 1's performance was at the lower limit of the scoring scales. So all age equivalencies appeared to be <1.00. Post-therapy the age equivalency for the Symbolic Play Test was several months in advance of scores on both language scales which were still around the lower limit of the scales.

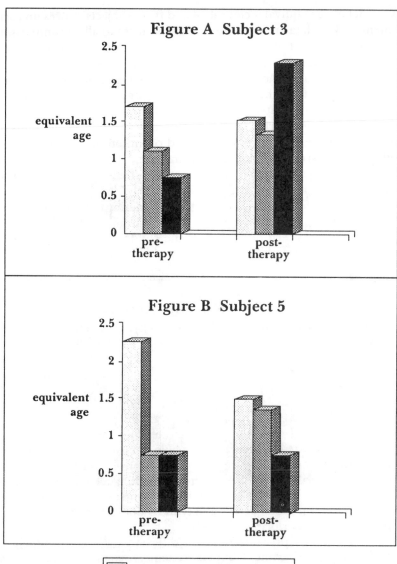

Figure A Subject 3

Figure B Subject 5

Symbolic Play
Expressive Language
Comprehension

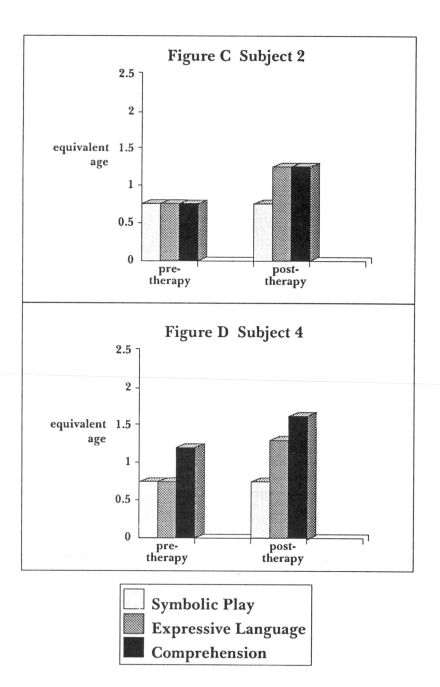

Figure C Subject 2

Figure D Subject 4

Symbolic Play
Expressive Language
Comprehension

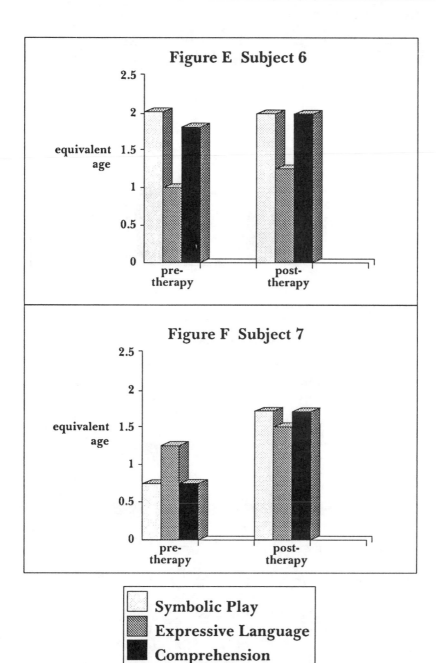

Figure E Subject 6

Figure F Subject 7

Symbolic Play
Expressive Language
Comprehension

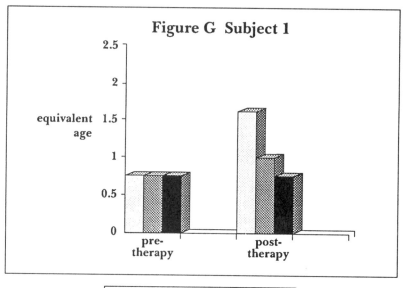

Figure G Subject 1

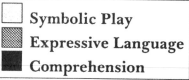

Symbolic Play

Expressive Language

Comprehension

Table 2 . Effect of therapy on the relationship between language and cognition.

Subject	Expression	Comprehension
1	-	-
2	(e)	(e)
3	r	e
4	(e)	(e)
5	r	-
6	r	r
7	r	e

Key	r	=	lag reduced
	e	=	lag eliminated
	(e)	=	lag not present on initial assessment but lead of language over cognition reduced
	-	=	lag not reduced or eliminated

Table 2 summarises the overall results of the study which allow comparison with Cunningham, Glenn, Wilkinson and Sloper's (1985) findings that for children with Down's Syndrome language skills develop more slowly than symbolic functioning. For five of the seven subjects (Subjects 2, 3, 5, 6, 7) linguistic skills changed more than cognitive functioning (as measured by the Symbolic Play Test) with one of these subjects (Subject 2) joining Subject 4 in having language performance on both expressive language and comprehension scales in advance of cognitive functioning. In only one subject (Subject 1) did post-therapy Symbolic Play Test performance remain as much in advance of language performance on both Reynell Developmental Language Scales as it had been on pre-therapy testing.

Discussion

The first point to note is the difficulty of obtaining accurate assessments of performance from this client group. Two main problems arose. First, several of the children were initially functioning at a level which was below or around the lower limit of the assessments which translated into an age equivalency such as '<1.00'. This meant that the initial performance could not be calculated exactly, and had implications for identifying and estimating change. The problem was compounded by those subjects whose test performance was variable and for whom clinical judgement would have predicted different scores. This is illustrated by the fact that three of the children (Subjects 3, 5 and 6) scored lower on the second Symbolic Play Test assessment than they had on initial testing. These considerations make it meaningless to calculate numerical comparisons of performance and thus the authors have looked for individual patterns of change.

The study took the form of individual case studies and the results are presented for individual children because the group was not homogenous in respect of, for example, age or profile of difficulties. The number of subjects was also very small allowing no conclusions to be drawn but nevertheless allowing some comments to be made about the efficacy of the speech therapy programme offered to these pre-school children with Down's Syndrome.

The results for individual subjects indicate that for five of the seven children in the study (Subjects 2, 3, 4, 6 7) both understanding and output of language improved more in relation to symbolic functioning than would have been expected according to the evidence presented in Cunningham, Glenn & Sloper's study. These positive findings provide support for the argument that the speech therapy programme provided had a beneficial effect for these subjects.

The change in Subject 5's performance was not as convincing as for some of the other children but although comprehension remained in the same relative relationship to cognition, the lag of expressive language behind symbolic play was reduced.

However, Subject 1, the youngest child in the study, did not follow the general trend and this can perhaps partially be explained by surmising that for such young children symbolic play and language are inextricably linked. The development of these two areas follows a very similar path and it is perhaps not possible, at an early age, to separate one from the other as the project sought to do. Repetition of this study with another group of children would help clarify this hypothesis.

Cunningham *et al.* had found that the difference between symbolic functioning and language increased with age and was more apparent for boys than girls. Our results did not support this. However, the subject group was very small and more similar age and sex-related changes to those found by Cunningham might be identified in a larger study. Within our results there was no suggestion of an age related effect: the older children did not seem to make less improvement on the language assessments than the younger ones nor did the girls do significantly better than the boys.

Whilst being very encouraged by the results, care has to be taken in their interpretation. It could be argued that the apparent benefits are not due to the specific nature of the speech therapy intervention but just to the interest of another professional. The 'Hawthorne Effect' is partially controlled for, however, as the children in the comparison study by Cunningham, Glenn, Wilkinson & Sloper were also having regular input from professionals. Thus we can have more confidence that the changes in speech and language were due, specifically, to the effect of the speech therapy programme.

Parents were invited to participate in all sessions. Parents' views were sought at the beginning of, and during the project, and the work was designed to meet the needs and issues raised. In the final instance only those parents involved can say whether they felt that the project met their general expectations of speech therapy and whether, specifically, the therapy programme met the needs of their individual child. However, an indication that expectations were met was provided by the excellent attendance rate during the study. The parents involved maintained a high level of commitment to the project which contributed to the positive results obtained.

From the outset evidence about the value of routines came from parents' observations. One mother reported a game she, her son (who had Down's Syndrome) and daughter played at lunch times. The younger girl enjoyed a routine which involved pointing to and naming objects around the room. This activity, when it had become familiar after several repetitions, proved interesting to the older boy who requested frequent repetitions and who was interested in the game for far longer than his younger sister. We suggest that the familiarity and predictability of the activity made this language game accessible. The tirelessness with which such games may be requested further supports the idea that routinised activity is not boring for the child.

Further evidence of language learning through routines came from one mother who described how she had regularly engaged in a game aimed at helping her daughter learn the word 'key'. Incidental to this activity was the use of the word 'door' and when she began to use 'door' her parents traced it back to the 'key-finding' routine. Reports such as these which come from those most involved with the child's language learning reinforced our belief in the value of Event Theory and routine for language learning.

Summary
Overall, the results indicate that this specific speech therapy programme led to a greater increase in language skills (both comprehension and expression) than would have been expected from a more general intervention programme. These are very positive findings, particularly in the light of the relatively small amount of speech therapy provided and the fact that very different (in age and ability) children showed evidence of change. Such a small scale study can only provide pointers to a fruitful area for further study. However, one clear implication is that language learning will be enhanced if attention is paid not only to the aims but also to the way in which children learn and may be helped to learn, language.

References

Bruner, J (1983). *Child's Talk*. Oxford University Press.

Cunningham, C, Glenn, S, Wilkinson, P and Sloper P (1985). Mental ability, symbolic play and receptive and expressive language of young children with Down's Syndrome. *Journal of Child Psychology and Psychiatry*, 26(2).

Dean, E C and Howell, J (1986). Developing Linguistic Awareness: a theoretically based approach to phonological disorders. *British Journal of Disorders of Communication*, 21.

Dean, E C Howell, J Hill A, and Waters D (1990). *The Metaphon Resource Pack*. NFER Nelson.

Dewart, H and Summers, S (1988). *The Pragmatics Profile of Early Communication Skills*. NFER Nelson.

Harris, J (1988). *Language Development in Schools for Children with Severe Learning Difficulties*. Croom Helm.

Howell, J and Dean, E C (1987).   Reflection and Learning in the Therapeutic Situation. *Journal of Child Language Teaching and Therapy*, 3(3) .

Howell, J and Dean, E C (1991).   *Treating Phonological Disorders in Children. Metaphon: Theory to Practice*. Far Communications.

Knowles, W and Masidlover M (1982). *The Derbyshire Language Scheme*. Derbyshire County Council.

Lowe, M and Costello, A J (1979). *The Symbolic Play Test*. NFER.

Nelson, K (1986). Event Knowledge and Cognitive Development. In Nelson, K (Ed). *Event Knowledge: Structure and Function in Development*. LEA.

Reynell, J. (1977) *Reynell Development Language Skills* (Revised). NFER.

Thurman, S (1989). *Speech Therapy with Pre-School Down's Syndrome Children*. Proceedings of College of Speech Therapists' Conference.

Wirz, S C M & Dean, E C (1990). *Revised Edinburgh Functional Communication Profile*. Communication Skill Builders.

Appendix 1

1.Build a relationship with the child.
On Joe's first visit the clinician asked his mother what toys Joe would like to play with and the session was spent with all three playing together. By the end of the session Joe was happy to play with the clinician on his own.

2.Carry out a comprehensive linguistic assessment covering, interaction, understanding and use of language; and the speech sound system (as appropriate).
On the second and third sessions Joe's performance in both testing and free play was recorded and analysed. During these sessions Joe worked with both his mother and the clinician.

3.Specify the linguistic factors which will determine the verbal input to the child and will influence the choice of routine.
Assessment indicated that Joe had some specific speech production problems in addition to demonstrating linguistic levels below his chronological age. The aim formulated for the clinician's input to Joe and as a guide:

     (a)   to build up awareness of sounds and the speech sound system.
     (b)   to encourage Joe to 'play' with speech sounds.
     (c)   to facilitate single word output in meaningful contexts.
     (d)   to develop comprehension of two word phrases ie, noun, verb (Teddy drink); noun, noun (Teddy cup).

4.In consultation with the caregiver choose a few routines to try.
The clinician and Joe's mother discussed a range of routines which were related to his everyday life, and which he found motivating. These included:

Setting out animals in a farm.	Feeding dolly.
Book routine.	Sound toys (rattles, pipes, bells, etc.).

5. Introduce the routines to the child to decide whether they prove motivating and interesting.
Three of the chosen routines proved particularly facilitating for Joe and these were adopted.
Setting out animals
Feeding dolly
Sound toys

6.Plan how the linguistic aims and routines can be assimilated.

Routine	Aims to be achieved
Sound toy routine	(a) and (b) (see above)
Feeding doll	(c) and (d)
Setting out animals	

7. Begin therapy with the child
Joe attended for therapy fortnightly. His mother was present for all sessions. This level of involvement allowed her to reinforce the therapeutic emphasis on a day to day basis. Her suggestions for modification of the routines and aims made in the light of her involvement were very valuable in ensuring that the work was maximally effective.

8. Re-assess the aims and choice of routine in the light of the child's response.
To maintain Joe's interest the linguistic demands within each routine were increased until such extension was no longer feasible. At this point new routines were negotiated and introduced. On average, the routines were changed after about 5 sessions (10 weeks) although this varied to some extent.

Motivational Deficits and their Relation to Learning Difficulties in Young Children with Down's Syndrome

Jennifer G Wishart

Introduction

This chapter provides an overview of findings from an on-going programme of research into the learning process in young children with Down's Syndrome. At this stage, the aims of the research are descriptive rather than prescriptive, with the main objective being to provide a detailed database on the nature and course of early learning in this particular group of children. The obvious longer-term aim of the research is to identify those teaching methods which can best help such children to achieve a higher level of success in their attempts at mastering their surroundings. We are especially concerned to find out why it is that so few children with learning difficulties manage to reap the full benefit from the limited skills that they do develop and also why it is that so many of them become such reluctant learners.

Our research programme has concentrated on children with Down's Syndrome for a number of reasons. The first, and most practical, is that Down's Syndrome is the most common cause of cognitive impairment in children, affecting around one third of those with severe learning difficulties. Approximately 1000 babies are born with Down's Syndrome every year in the UK alone. There is little evidence that prenatal screening programmes are having any major impact on this incidence rate and significant advances in health care, particularly in cardiology and immunology, mean that most children can now be expected to live long and relatively healthy lives. A direct result of this is that the number of individuals in the community with this particular disability has increased fourfold over recent decades.

Many of the health problems commonly associated with Down's Syndrome (e.g. heart disease, respiratory problems, auditory/visual impairment) can now be successfully managed. Little progress has been made, however, in alleviating the learning difficulties which almost invariably accompany this genetic disorder. The degree of mental handicap experienced can vary enormously: a small percentage of children suffer profound handicap while others are moderately or only mildly handicapped by their condition (Rynders et al., 1978; Carr, 1985). It is this variation in developmental outcome that provided a second reason for focusing on this particular subgroup of children with learning difficulties. Down's Syndrome itself - Trisomy 21 - results from the presence in triplicate (rather than duplicate) of chromosome 21 and is one of the few mentally-handicapping conditions for which precise aetiology is known (Patterson, 1987). Individual children obviously inherit very different combinations of genes from each of their biological parents but with the exception of rare cases of mosaicism, every child with Down's Syndrome will have exactly the same genetic imbalance in all body cells. As we have just seen, however, Down's Syndrome has no uniform impact on developmental progress and there is also a notable absence of the usual strong relationship between the IQs of the children and the IQs and socio-economic status of their parents (Gibson, 1978). Together these facts make it highly probable that at least some of the variation in the level and kinds of skills achieved by individual children is determined by psychological factors. This means that although the learning difficulties experienced in Down's Syndrome may have thus far proved to be unresponsive to medical intervention, there is reason to believe that they could still prove to be responsive to psychologically-based methods of intervention.

To have any chance of success, any psychological attempt at intervention in Down's Syndrome will need to be very well grounded in an understanding of the exact nature of developmental processes in this group of children. However, a very major - and perhaps surprising - obstacle stands in the way of any attempt at facilitative intervention: the incompleteness of our knowledge of psychological development in Down's Syndrome children. It is over 130 years since Langdon Down first described this syndrome and yet we still know remarkably little about the actual *process* of learning in Down's Syndrome. Our lack of knowledge in this area is not due to any shortage of psychological studies of children with Down's Syndrome. Some would in fact maintain that this group of children have had more than their fair share of research attention. Much of the research carried out to date, however, has been cross-sectional and has focused only on the end products of learning and not on its dynamics. Many studies, moreover, have only succeeded in demonstrating what was already fairly obvious: that in comparison to any non-handicapped child of a similar age, a child with Down's Syndrome will generally perform very poorly on most cognitive tasks and will be late in achieving the important milestones in cognitive development.

Only longitudinal studies can provide any real insights into developmental processes but very few longitudinal studies have been carried out with children with Down's Syndrome. This is no doubt partly because of the time and costliness of any long-term study of a population in whom development is so slow to unfold. It also stems, however, from a basic lack of recognition of the need for a separate database on development in this group of children. This in turn stems from the fact that a great deal of past research carried out with children with Down's Syndrome has prejudged the very issues which it should have been addressing by simply assuming that development in handicap is basically similar in nature to -

and can therefore be fully understood in terms of - normal developmental processes. At first glance, this may seem to be an appropriate and scientific approach to studying children with learning difficulties, one which would allow us to take advantage of our hard-won knowledge of normal developmental processes in trying to understand exactly what it is that goes wrong in such children. Recent studies suggest, however, that development in handicapped children may be quite different in its structure and organisation from that seen in normal development (Morss, 1985; Wishart, 1988).

The assumption that development in children with a learning disability is simply a slowed-down, less efficient version of normal development is rooted in the very vocabulary usually used to describe such children - terms such as 'retarded', 'developmentally delayed', or 'slow learners'. The uncritical acceptance of a 'slow' theory of development in handicap is also reflected in the widespread use of psychometrically-derived tests to assess the developmental status of children with learning disabilities and in experimental studies which 'match' groups of handicapped and non-handicapped children in order to study some aspect of their learning. Grouping children in terms of their 'mental ages' assumes that they can be considered to be at an equivalent stage in their cognitive development and to have similar ability profiles. This may be a convenient assumption but it can often be far from accurate. On most MA tests any given score can be achieved by any one of a number of combinations of successes and failures on individual test items. This makes equivalence a risky assumption even in the case of two children of a similar age but clearly an even riskier assumption in the case of two children of 'matched' mental ages but very differing chronological ages, as is generally the case when a child with Down's Syndrome is matched with a normally-developing child. Any two such children are very likely to have very differing sets of skills.

Even when 'matched' children *do* have similar ability profiles, there can still be problems. Mental age scores take no account of how the skills being measured have been acquired. By the very nature of their design, psychometric tests assume that each child will have acquired their repertoire of skills by the same route and in the same progression, the only difference being that the acquisition process will have taken longer in the case of the handicapped child. This leads into perhaps the most crucial problem with this type of approach - the assumption that test performance is a reasonably accurate reflection of the skills available to the child and that all children are equally motivated to demonstrate their skills in a test situation. Intuition alone would suggest that the child whose learning experience has been characterised by repeated and frequent failure might well approach a situation which is clearly designed to test the limits of their abilities in a different way to a child whose experience of success and failure has been more favourable. The learning history of an eight year old child with Down's Syndrome with a mental age of four, for example, is unlikely to bear much resemblance to that of an average four year old. Whereas a normal four year old child may enjoy showing off his/her skills, experience indicates that the eight year old with Down's Syndrome is far more likely to view any 'IQ'-type test as yet another test aimed at finding out what s/he can*not* do. Matches like this are nevertheless typical in much of the research carried out into learning in Down's Syndrome children.

Detailed study of the test behaviour of children with Down's Syndrome and longitudinal studies of the progression of development in this group of children are increasingly suggesting that development may follow quite different pathways in cases of handicap. The assumption that development in handicap is basically similar to the straightforward, incremental process described in normal developmental theory is beginning to seem very unsound. In particular it would seem that the link between competence and performance may be far from stable in this group of children and that many children may be underperforming both in test situations and in the classroom (see e.g. Duffy, 1991; Duffy & Wishart, 1987: Wishart & Duffy, 1990).

The three studies to be outlined below were carried out with the specific aim of providing a better understanding of the nature of the difficulties faced by children with Down's Syndrome at different stages in their development in learning new skills. The studies also aimed to investigate how early negative learning experience might affect the way in which subsequent learning is approached by this group of children. The studies also hoped to provide some insight into whether different methods of teaching might help to overcome some of these learning difficulties or could at least help such children to make better use of those abilities which we know them to be capable of acquiring.

Before describing the research, it is first worth making one very general point. Our research, as we have said, has focused almost exclusively on Down's Syndrome children - because of the relatively large number of children available for study and because of the known aetiology of their handicap. At a psychological level, however, many of the problems met by children with Down's Syndrome must be very similar to those faced by any child with an equivalent level of intellectual impairment, whatever its origins. This makes it likely that some of the avoidance strategies we have observed in Down's Syndrome children in response to what can at best be described as adverse learning experience may well be typical of other children with learning difficulties and have the same long-term developmental consequences. Specific studies would of course need to be carried out to test the legitimacy of any such extension of the findings. The last of the studies presented below describes our own first attempt at addressing this question. It compared the effectiveness of an errorless learning procedure for teaching discrimination skills to two groups of children with learning disabilities, a Down's Syndrome and a non-Down's Syndrome group. As will be seen, the results suggest that although there were some basic similarities between the two groups, there were also some important differences in how they responded to this approach.

Three studies of learning and development in infants and young children with Down's Syndrome

The three studies to be described looked at learning in children with Down's Syndrome aged between birth and sixteen years. The first two studies were long-term, longitudinal studies involving large groups of pre-school children; the third involved older children and was of smaller scale and shorter duration. Each of these studies has been described elsewhere in greater detail than will be possible here but it is hoped that the outline accounts to be given here will be sufficient to illustrate some of the factors which may be inhibiting the learning process in children with Down's Syndrome. Further information on design, methodology and the findings can be readily obtained from the original sources.

The sample studied represented over 90% of children with Down's Syndrome in the Lothian region of Scotland and was representative of that total population in all important respects (such as associated health problems, socio-economic status, number of siblings). All of the children who took part had been volunteered by their parents. The research nature of the studies was fully explained in order that no child was volunteered on the misunderstanding that the studies were intervention studies or in the belief that participation would be of direct or immediate benefit to the child. It was, of course, possible to assure parents that the research would in no way be harmful to their child's development and that s/he was likely to enjoy taking part. Parents in general seemed very willing to volunteer their child on the basis that the information collected in the studies would hopefully be of future use to other children with Down's Syndrome.

a. A longitudinal study of the development of the object concept.

Our first study looked at development of the object concept over the first five years of life. This is a very important step in early cognitive development, one that is normally achieved within the first two years by infants who are not cognitively impaired. Previous research had already shown that Down's Syndrome children even at school age still had difficulties with many of the hiding tasks used to measure object concept development in infancy (Wohlheuter & Sindberg, 1975). At the time of carrying out this research, no intensive study of this area of development had been carried out with pre-school children or infants with Down's Syndrome, the reasoning presumably being that if older children had problems with these tasks, then younger children would inevitably have the same or greater problems. It is perhaps useful to explain first what is meant by the term 'object concept development'. It is now over 50 years since the Swiss psychologist Piaget first observed that the understanding of objects in infancy goes through a regular, invariant sequence of development (Piaget, 1937). Learning about the nature and properties of objects is basic to understanding even the simplest of commonplace events. It is particularly central to understanding the physical laws which govern interactions between objects and between objects and people - the laws of space, time and causality. Many theorists believe that the early acquisition of a concept of objects is basic to the development of reasoning and logical thought at older ages; yet others maintain that it is an essential prerequisite for language development (although there is considerable disagreement over both claims).

Although there is considerable theoretical disarray over the exact significance of object concept development to cognitive development in general, there is widespread scientific agreement that infants *do* have considerable problems in understanding objects. Given how many amazing abilities have recently been uncovered in infants, it may at first seem hard to accept that infants do not initially think of objects in the same way as adults do and have to go through a laborious apprenticeship to learn even the most basic facts about objects and their properties. A vast array of carefully-conducted experiments, however, confirms that young infants initially do have enormous difficulties in understanding such things, Every infant - no matter how clever s/he may be - has to learn, for example, that two objects which look the same but are seen in different places at the same time are in reality two different objects; they also have to learn that if one object is placed inside another, it will share the movements of that object, even although it was not itself seen to change position. These difficulties can easily be demonstrated by presenting infants with apparently simple hiding tasks on which they will reliably make very odd but predictable errors.

Infants' responses to tasks in which objects are hidden in various ways have revealed six clear stages in object concept development, each associated with specific search errors. At the two lowest levels, the infant is required to search visually for an object that has disappeared from sight (e.g. to follow the trajectory of a ball which has been dropped); the four higher-level tasks require search for an object which has been hidden in some way (e.g. an attractive toy which has been hidden under one of two identical paper cups). The complexity of the hiding sequence increases with each level of task - see Figure 1. Because there is always a 50% probability of chance success in the higher level tasks (there are, after all, only two possible locations for the hidden object), a number of trials of each task are usually presented (generally 4 or 6). The infant must succeed on all of these to be credited with having reached that stage in development of the object concept.

D

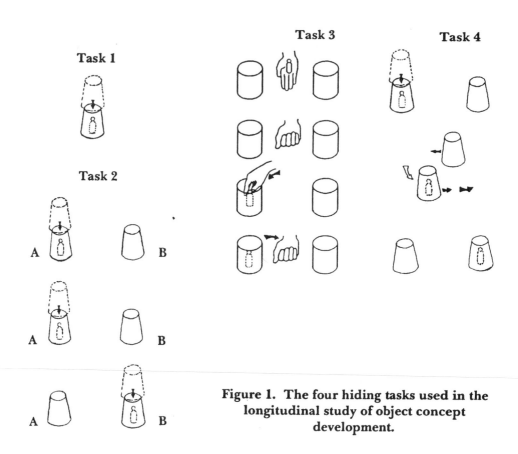

Figure 1. The four hiding tasks used in the longitudinal study of object concept development.

Our research aimed to chart the development of each of the four highest object concept stages in children with Down's Syndrome and to investigate how each new step in this learning was approached. In order to avoid making any prior assumptions about what the children would or would not be able to do at any given age, we adopted a design in which all children were presented with four trials of each of the four levels of task at each age of testing. The very low motor skill demands of object concept testing made this feasible for even the youngest subjects we planned to test (3-6 month olds): object concept testing does not require the child to be able to sit unsupported (they can sit on their mother's lap) and reaching does not need to be highly skilled, only clear in its direction.

Our previous cross-sectional work with a large group of non-handicapped infants (N=228) had already established the developmental norms for success on Tasks 1, 2, 3 and 4 to be 5, 10, 15 and 22+ months respectively (Wishart & Bower, 1984). This study was to be semi-longitudinal, with subjects entering the study at different ages and being tested every two weeks on all four of the tasks. Since earlier work had indicated that repeated exposure to these tests can accelerate development to some degree (but without affecting the order in which stages were acquired), we added a control group of normally-developing children into the study; these children were presented with the same tests on the same schedule as the Down's Syndrome subjects. The criterion adopted for achieving each stage was success on all four trials of the relevant task on two consecutive testing sessions.

Fifty children with Down's Syndrome participated in the study although not all provided developmental data on acquisition of each of the four stages of object concept development (since this depended on age and developmental stage at time of entry to the study). Age of entry to the study ranged between four months and five years. The study was run in two parts, with the three to five year olds being tested first. At this age level, it was expected that the non-handicapped control children would be well beyond the stages of object concept development being studied but that the majority of the Down's Syndrome children would not yet be able to pass the higher-level tasks. This was indeed the pattern which emerged in the first testing sessions: performance in these subjects was in fact very poor on all levels of task, whereas the control children appeared to find all of the tasks very simple. Subsequent testing sessions provided a surprise, however. The scores of the Down's Syndrome children were found to increase dramatically over repeat sessions whereas the performance of the non-handicapped children was found to deteriorate significantly.

A number of factors proved to be responsible for these contrasting patterns. It was, for example, very clear from the accompanying comments of the control subjects that elaborate teasing often underlay their 'poor' performance in later testing sessions and that it was not due to any drastic drop in ability; correct search was easily restored by cajoling or by hiding chocolate rather than a toy. It was impossible to judge whether teasing was similarly responsible for the initially poor performance of the children with Down's Syndrome. Because of their very low levels of expressive language, it was far less easy to determine whether their lack of success was also a case of 'won't do' rather than 'can't do' but as cajoling or bribery did not lead to better performance, this suggests that their failures in early sessions were in fact genuine. The overall improvement shown by this group within just two months, however, was quite remarkable. This sequence of development, it will be recalled, normally takes two years to unfurl in children without any learning disability.

Table 1.
Results for younger subjects in longitudinal study of object concept development.

	Age (in months) of achievement of success on hiding tasks 1-4			
DS subjects:				
	Task 1	**Task 2**	**Task 3**	**Task 4**
Mean Age	7.75	10.50	19.25	18.00
Range	6.25 - 10.75	7.25 - 14.00	14.50 - 26.75	11.00 - 25.25
Non-handicapped subjects:				
Cross-sectional normative data (Bower & Wishart, 1984)				
Age at which				
75% of Ss	5.00	10.00	15.00	22+
passed				
Longitudinal data (control group)				
Mean Age	4.75	7.75	12.25	14.50
Range	4.00 - 5.75	4.75 - 8.50	9.25 - 14.25	10.25 - 17.00

Note: All months have been rounded up to nearest 0.25

(from Wishart, 1990)

      Results from the younger Down's Syndrome subjects helped to cast some light on this rather odd pattern . Table 1 shows the mean age of first success on each of the four tasks for the younger subject groups. Although, as was expected, the children with Down's Syndrome were slower than the non-handicapped children in achieving success on most (but notably, not all) of the tasks, for many subjects age of first achievement of success on each of the four tasks was either within or close to the normal age range for solving these tasks. It could be argued that this was only achieved by virtue of the extra experience given with these tasks but this in itself does not detract materially from the fact that this group of children with Down's Syndrome had proved themselves capable of reaching these cognitive levels by these ages.

      Far less encouraging was the subsequent developmental history of each newly-acquired skill. Not long after success had first been achieved on each level of task, errors soon reappeared. Although the Down's Syndrome infants often seemed to be sufficiently motivated and searched quickly for the hidden toys, they frequently made errors on tasks which by then should have been relatively easy for them; they would look surprised at these errors but often would not bother to correct them. Introducing chocolate met with some success in restoring performance in the immediate post-acquisition weeks but proved to be ineffective in later weeks. By then the poor performance of these subjects seemed to truly reflect a competence that had deteriorated beyond retrieval rather than just a loss of motivation or inadequate attention to the task. Control subjects, by contrast, generally worked hard at each level of task in all sessions, regardless of whether the task in hand was above or below their current developmental status. Once success had been achieved on any given task, it was usually reliably reproduced in subsequent testing sessions.

Taking the results from the two age groups together, two conclusions can be drawn. Firstly, it would appear that infants with Down's Syndrome have higher levels of cognitive ability than would be predicted from typical performance at older ages on the same cognitive tasks. Secondly, it would seem that the consolidation of new learning may be a major problem for children with Down's Syndrome. When the extent and rate of improvement in performance over sessions in the older group is taken into consideration with the ages of initial achievement of each stage in object concept development and the subsequent instability of these achievements in the younger group, the interpretation that the older group were reacquiring the understanding necessary to pass these tasks is difficult to avoid. It would seem that they may have had to re-tune their earlier learning because of failure to consolidate it adequately at the time of initial acquisition.

One last point is worth making here in relation to the behaviour of the Down's Syndrome children in this particular test setting. We have seen that the children often made unexpected errors on very easy tasks even when they were apparently attending carefully and seemed keen to retrieve the toy. There were also, however, a great many instances in which children 'switched out' of the tasks and therefore simply failed by default. This opting out occurred at a number of levels and took a variety of forms. Some children, for example, just swept both cups off the table while looking at neither. Others repeatedly chose the same cup on every trial, a low-level strategy but one which leads to success on half of the trials (but overall results in a 'fail' score). One of the most commonly-adopted strategies was to use - or more accurately, *misuse* - a particular social skill to get out of the task in hand - for example, by producing a party-trick (such as blowing raspberries) or by refusing to watch the hiding sequence, instead locking the experimenter into eye contact while all the time smiling broadly at her. At best, this sort of behaviour led to a delay in search, thereby increasing the difficulty of the task by introducing a memory component; at worst, it could result in no search response being made at all within the time period allowed for search. These types of avoidance strategies were not randomly produced nor were they simply a reflection of boredom or fatigue with the hiding tasks. They were as likely to be produced at an early stage in testing as at later stages and were strongly associated with the level of difficulty of the task currently being presented. Low-level strategy responding tended to be produced on what should have been the easier tasks whereas the deliberate avoidance behaviours were produced more often on the more difficult tasks. Other tasks were unaffected, even although they involved the same toys and cups and required the same kind of search behaviours. (For a fuller description of these studies and their results see Wishart, 1987; 1988; 1990).

b. A developmental investigation of operant learning.

In order to investigate these counterproductive behaviours more closely, we decided to look directly at the learning process itself. We also narrowed the focus to the very youngest age levels in the hope of identifying the origins of the avoidance strategies we had seen being repeatedly produced.

We decided to use an operant learning paradigm to investigate how much the ratio of success to failure experienced during learning affected the rate of that learning. We also hoped to identify which ratio of success to failure promoted the most active exploration of a learning situation. Because of the hypotonia often present in the early months, an operant task requiring minimal motor skills was chosen. Infants sat securely in a baby seat in such a position that a 60 degree kick of the foot broke a lightbeam, triggering a 1-second rotation of a brightly-coloured mobile: the task was to detect the contingency between this activity and the movements of the mobile. The criterion we adopted for successful operant learning was a 1.5 increase in kicking rate during reinforcement periods, maintained for two out of three consecutive minutes. (A fuller description of the methodology of the operant learning studies and of findings from them can be found in Wishart, 1990; 1991).

Fifty infants with Down's Syndrome aged between one month and two years took part in the original pilot work and in the final cross-sectional and longitudinal studies. The original intention was to run full control groups of non-handicapped children matched both for chronological age and for mental age in order to allow us to identify any changes in responsiveness to the task's parameters which were related to age (mental or chronological) and/or amount of task experience. It proved to be impossible, however, to collect sufficient comparative data from control subjects aged greater than nine months. Although most of the subjects with Down's Syndrome proved to be happy to sit through the eighteen minute procedure at all age levels, the older control subjects simply refused to tolerate the experimental situation for more than a few minutes. This difference in cooperation levels is in itself interesting particularly as it held even when mental age was taken into consideration (see Table 2). The inadequacy of mental age measures has already been discussed and the findings from this study add weight to the criticism that such measures provide only a very limited basis for subject matching. The differences in cooperation which were so clearly demonstrated could also not be explained by differences between subjects in the two groups on *non*-cognitive skills, such as mobility. Many of the older subjects with Down's Syndrome used in this study were already mobile by the age of testing and thus equally capable of showing that they did not want to continue by simply getting up and walking away. Very few did so, however - or even indicated any degree of discontent at being kept in the same situation for this relatively lengthy period. Cooperation in a learning context is often taken as a positive sign but it was clear from the response patterns of the two groups in this particular situation that this is not the only interpretation (see below).

Table 2.
Mean time (minutes) spent by different subject groups in two testing sessions.

Age Level	Session	Subjects		
		Down's Syndrome	MA -matched	CA-matched
6 months	1	14.13	10.00	11.00
	2	15.75	7.25	11.75
12 months	1	14.50	10.25	3.25
	2	14.38	7.13	1.25
18 months	1	15.88	2.63	1.00
	2	14.20	1.13	0.25
24 months	1	13.50	1.13	0.00
	2	12.50	0.88	0.00

(from Wishart, 1991)

The study itself investigated the effects of both contingent and non-contingent reinforcement schedules on learning activity. In the contingent schedules, the mobile rotated if - and only if - the infant kicked through the beam. In mixed contingent/non-contingent schedules, a set number of 'free' rotations were also delivered at random intervals by a microcomputer. The aim was to see whether providing different levels of self-generated success (100% v 80%) had differential effects on learning speed and also to investigate whether provision of non-contingent reinforcement helped or hindered the learning process. Analysis of the data from these studies is not yet complete but already some interesting developmental patterns have clearly emerged:

   a.   with increasing age, infants with Down's Syndrome rely increasingly on reinforcement being generated by others, even when able to generate higher rates of 'reward' by themselves,

   b.   this dependence can be reduced and infants can be encouraged to exercise their own control over the situation by enhancing the success rate they initially experience during learning,

   c.   enhancing the level of control experienced in early learning can lead to better consolidation of that learning.

The finding that children with Down's Syndrome increasingly look to others to take the initiative in their learning adds to the evidence from the object concept studies that young children with Down's Syndrome in many ways may add to their already-existing handicap by failing to make the best use of their own abilities in problem-solving situations. Children with Down's Syndrome seem to learn very quickly that help will often be on hand and will be given even if their own attempts at finding a solution are fairly half-hearted. Holding back in difficult learning situations may be an understandable response in a child for whom even the best attempts at trying to learn a new skill are likely to be met with repeated failure. However, indiscriminately provided support may well have the opposite effect to that intended - it may simply encourage the child to relinquish the initiative in learning and to reduce their own input in direct proportion to the support being given (see Figure 2).

Figure 2. Operant learning

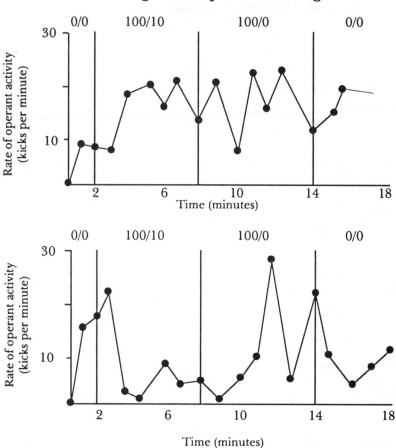

Figure 2 compares performance of a nine-month old infant with DS (upper graph) with performance on the same operant learning task one year later (lower graph). The reinforcement schedules in operation in each of the four time sections were:

1.   **0/0** - 0% contingent reinforcement for kicks. 0% "free", computer-generated (base period).

2.   **100/10** - 100% contingent reinforcement for kicks. 10% "free", computer-generated reinforcement.

3.   100/0 -   100% contingent reinforcement for kicks. 0% "free", computer-generated reinforcement .

4.   0/0   - as 1 (Extinction period).

At nine months, the infant performed well under both reinforcement schedules. When older, however, he quickly gave up kicking when 10% free reinforcement was provided even though his subsequent performance showed clearly that he was capable of producing higher levels of reinforcement for himself.

(from Wishart, 1990)

Parents may often - for the best of reasons but with possibly the worst of effects - help their children to success on tasks which they are trying to teach them. They may also often reward them simply for trying, regardless of how close to the desired behaviour the child's response actually was. This combination of high levels of non-contingent reinforcement and low levels of self-generated reinforcement must make it even more difficult for the child with a learning disability to detect any consistent relationship between what he does and what happens around him. It would not therefore be surprising if in these circumstances the child becomes a reluctant learner, happy to allow others to carry the load in new learning situations.

c. A comparison of the efficiency of two different methods of teaching discrimination skills.

This set of studies differs from those described thus far in two ways: firstly, it involved children with Down's Syndrome of much older ages and secondly, it investigated the learning process by studying how children respond to two methods of teaching, each placing quite different emphasis on the role of erring in learning. The focus in these studies was therefore on the children's response to errors, rather than to success.

Thirty-two children aged between six and sixteen years took part in two studies, one of which compared the response of Down's Syndrome and normally-developing children to the two teaching strategies, the other of which compared the response of children with Down's Syndrome and children who had equivalent levels of learning disabilities but of different aetiology. The latter study also looked at the long-term stability of any learning resulting from the application of the errorless teaching strategy.

The skills being taught were shape and nonsense figure discrimination, the latter being included to control for any effects of prior positive or negative experience with the target stimuli (none of the children could possibly have seen any of the nonsense figures being used). All subjects were trained on both shape and nonsense figure tasks, a counterbalanced design leading to one teaching strategy being applied on one task, the other on the second. (A fuller account of the design of these studies can be found in Duffy & Wishart, 1987; Duffy, 1990).

Figure 3. Examples of errorless learning test cards
(shape discrimination - rectangle)

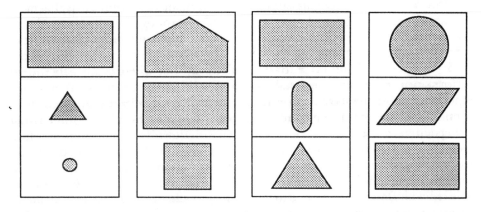

(from Duffy & Wishart, 1987)

The two teaching methods we compared were based on trial-and-error and errorless learning. The major difference between the two was that the first allowed the children to err as often as would be usual in learning any new task while the second 'protected' them from experiencing a large number of errors during the learning process. On each trial, the child was shown three test cards, each depicting a shape or nonsense figure, and asked to point out the selected target. An example of one of the sets of cards is given in Figure 3. In the standard trial-and-error approach, correct responses were verbally praised. Incorrect responses were negatively reinforced, with children being told: "No, that is not right. Try again the next time." In the errorless procedure, the two competing shapes were 'faded in' over trials. In the very earliest trials, the card with the target shape was presented alongside two absolutely blank cards; in subsequent trials, the two alternative stimuli were initially much smaller than the target stimulus but increased gradually in size with each trial. Again, children were verbally praised if they made the correct choice. Errors were not commented on but instead of proceeding with the next trial, the previous trial was re-presented, with this procedure being repeated as necessary until the child had shown mastery of each step in the training sequence.

A number of useful findings emerged from these studies. For both the normally-developing and Down's Syndrome children, errorless learning proved to be the superior strategy, both during training and in post-tests. When the trial-and-error training was used, however, the children with Down's Syndrome were very poor in both absolute and relative terms. We were not surprised to find this. Trial and error learning is the form of learning which corresponds most closely to the conditions encountered in natural, everyday learning situations and children with Down's Syndrome are reliably poor learners under such conditions. However, the experimental design had been balanced to control for the effects of order of experience of the two teaching strategies and an interesting differential effect of order of presentation emerged in the Down's Syndrome group. For those children given trial-and-error training first, an *adverse* effect on subsequent performance in the errorless task was found; in those given initial errorless experience, subsequent trial-and-error performance was *enhanced*. No such effect of order was present in the control subjects. This suggests that experience of erring depresses the performance of children with Down's Syndrome in a learning context. It also indicates that an errorless approach might counteract this effect to some degree. Experience of errorless learning appeared to have served a 'priming' function in this study, apparently increasing the motivation of the children with Down's Syndrome to tackle the trial-and-error task. This could be because their experience of learning in the errorless context had demonstrated to them that they *were* capable of learning the sorts of skills required for success on tasks of this type.

The success shown by the children with Down's Syndrome on these discrimination tasks was highly encouraging, especially given that only one brief errorless training session had been used. Our second, follow-up study aimed therefore to investigate the longevity of these new discriminative skills. It also sought to investigate whether the newly acquired skills could be demonstrated in the absence of the supporting framework of errorless experience and whether children with other forms of learning disability would respond equally positively to errorless training. The study took place over a six week period. Although the teachers had indicated that all of the children usually required several lessons when being taught similar skills using conventional methods, the majority of children in both groups demonstrated that they could learn the target discrimination within a single training session when an errorless procedure was adopted. They also demonstrated that they could retain that learning over six weeks.

The two groups of learning disabled children had been matched for mental age level prior to taking part in this study. This matching was done both on the basis of teachers' assessments of classroom performance and from the children's scores on a standard IQ test (the Kaufman Assessment Battery for Children). Once again, despite 'matching', a clear difference emerged between the response of the two groups to the introduction of an errorless training procedure: in the first training session, the children with Down's Syndrome required significantly fewer training trials to acquire the discrimination than the non-Down's Syndrome children. No differences appeared in any subsequent sessions, however. This quicker learning by the subjects with Down's Syndrome, when taken in conjunction with the absence of any between-groups differential in pre/post test improvement scores in this first session, supports the interpretation that the children with Down's Syndrome responded more positively to errorless training *per se* rather than any suggestion that they may have started with an inherent advantage in discriminatory ability.

The results from these errorless learning studies are very encouraging but should not be taken as demonstrating that an errorless teaching strategy is effective in terms of learning *per se*. All-correct performance on a discrimination task does not necessarily imply that any actual discrimination *skill* has been acquired. Indeed our subsequent studies unfortunately confirmed that the errorless training had had no intrinsic learning value since there was no transfer of skill to a second task involving a different discrimination but requiring the same basic discrimination skills. There was even some evidence of negative transfer in some of the children we tested.

Why should this be? Poor transferability of discrimination skills could have resulted from the failure of an errorless technique to provide sufficiently detailed stimuli in order to distinguish them from the target stimulus: a fading procedure and then a recognition process guide choice. In essence then, what the subject is being taught is the correct choice but not why the remaining two are not correct; a task-specific strategy emerges, but one that is clearly of little use in any other situation. It is this omission which has led some to caution against the over-use of this technique (e.g. Dweck, 1975). While there seems good reason to believe that repeated experience of error produces poorly motivated learners, this does not mean that eliminating all experience of error is necessarily beneficial. The outside world is in any case not so user-friendly. An error-free approach in the classroom may therefore prepare the child poorly for real-life learning.

Conclusion

The studies outlined above have used a number of different methods to investigate learning in children with Down's Syndrome of various ages. The studies using the youngest subjects uncovered surprisingly high levels of initial ability but also demonstrated that this ability was put to very inefficient use. An increasing tendency to opt out of difficult learning with increasing age was observed, a tendency that is perhaps understandable given the unfavourable ratio of success to failure that children with Down's Syndrome must typically experience. Avoiding learning, however, can only add to the learning difficulties that children with

Down's Syndrome already face. It is therefore important that we seek to identify which methods of teaching will allow Down's Syndrome children to appreciate from the very earliest stages in development that they *are* capable of learning and that perseverance can ultimately be rewarding. It is also important that we do not allow children with Down's Syndrome to become over-dependent on others and encourage them to take the initiative in exploring each new learning situation to the fullness of their own abilities.

Supporting children with Down's Syndrome in their attempts to master their surroundings and to gain basic academic skills will require the evolution of teaching methods that respond to and supplement the particular learning 'style' of this group of children. This style seems to be greatly susceptible to motivational fluctuations and to be easily undermined by adverse learning experience. This chapter has not attempted to offer any firm predictions as to what the best methods may turn out to be. By describing behaviour in a variety of testing situations, our research has aimed to highlight the existence of important differences in the way that these children go about learning and to show how they often fail to make full use of many of the new skills they finally do acquire. The existence of significant differences in the learning process in children with Down's Syndrome implies that any new teaching method derived solely from theories of normal development is unlikely to meet with any great success since any straightforward adaptation of already-existing methods is likely to fail to meet the specific needs of the child with Down's Syndrome. It is to be hoped that future research will succeed in clarifying the functional relationship between competence and performance in this group of children. Only then shall we be in a position to help each child to reach his or her full potential in the most efficient - and enjoyable - way.

References

Carr, J (1985). The development of intelligence. In D Lane & B Stratford (eds). *Current Approaches to Down's Syndrome*. Holt, Rinehart & Winston.

Duffy, L (1990). *The relationship between competence and performance in early development in children with Down's Syndrome.* Unpublished Ph.D. dissertation, University of Edinburgh.

Duffy, L and Wishart, J G (1987). A comparison of two procedures for teaching discrimination skills to Down's Syndrome and non-handicapped children. *British Journal of Educational Psychology*, 57.

Dweck, C (1975). The role of expectations and attributions in the alleviation of learned helplessness. *Journal of Personality and Social Psychology*, 31.

Gibson, D (1978). *Down's Syndrome: The Psychology of Mongolism.* Cambridge University Press.

Morss, J R (1985). Early cognitive development - difference or delay? In D Lane & B Stratford (eds). *Current Approaches to Down's Syndrome*. Holt, Rinehart & Winston.

Patterson, D (1987). The causes of Down Syndrome. *Scientific American*, 257.

Piaget, J (1955). *The Construction of Reality*. Routledge & Kegan, Paul. (original French edition).

Rynders, J E, Spiker, D & Horrobin, J M (1978). Underestimating the educability of Down's Syndrome children. *American Journal of Mental Deficiency*, 82.

Wishart, J G & Bower, T G R (1984). Spatial relations and the object concept: a normative study. In L P Lipsitt and C K Rovee-Collier (eds). *Advances in Infancy Research: Vol.3*. Ablex.

Wishart, J G (1987). Performance of 3-5 year old Down's Syndrome and non-handicapped children on Piagetian infant search tasks. *American Journal of Mental Deficiency*, 92.

Wishart, J G (1988). Early learning in infants and young children with Down's Syndrome. In L Nadel (ed). *The Psychobiology of Down Syndrome*. M.I.T. Press.

Wishart, J G and Duffy, L (1990). Instability of performance on cognitive tests in infants and young children with Down's Syndrome. *British Journal of Educational Psychology*, 59.

Wishart, J G (1990). Learning to learn: the difficulties faced by infants and young children with Down's Syndrome. In Fraser, W I (ed). *Key Issues in Research in Mental Retardation*. Routledge.

Wishart, J G. (1991). Taking the initiative in learning: a developmental investigation of infants with Down's Syndrome. *International Journal of Disability, Development and Education*, 38.

Wohlheuter, M and Sindberg, R (1975). Longitudinal development of object permanence in mentally retarded children. *American Journal of Mental Deficiency*, 79.

Gentle Teaching for
Challenging Behaviour

Sally E Cheseldine

> Every human encounter validates or invalidates some or all of the
> participants in it. None is neutral. In the 'helping professions'.....each
> encounter typically validates the professional (as giving something of
> value) and invalidates the client (as receiving something of value).

> Thomas S Szasz (1973)

Introduction

In the field of severe learning difficulties one can quickly gain the impression that
much time is spent in pursuit of a Holy Grail, namely *the* way of achieving behavioural
order and cooperation. The idea that such a 'right way' exists is perhaps
perpetuated by the development of packages for intervention, such as the EDY
workshops (Foxen and McBrien, 1981), or the Portage model (Bluma *et al.*, 1977).
For the new arrival to the area of 'Challenging Behaviour' this can result in either
confusion, or in a naive belief that once the right recipe book has been purchased
then everything will fall into place. In which direction should one turn? On the
one hand there are numerous articles extolling the virtues of apparently rigid
behavioural procedures (Jordan, Singh and Repp, 1989), while on the other there
are those championing the cause of an 'ordinary life', with an emphasis on
environmental and social change (Blunden and Allen, 1987).

The argument in favour of punishment as an integral part of intervention
programmes somewhat surprisingly continues with vigour (Mulik, 1990), but
there has been increasing interest in approaches which aim to provide alternatives
to punishment as a way of meeting the challenge of difficult behaviour (Lovett,
1985; La Vigna and Donellan, 1986). The concept of 'Gentle Teaching' (McGee,
Menolascino, Hobbs and Menousek, 1987) as a non-aversive approach to helping
people with severe learning difficulties has perhaps received more attention than
most, possibly because of its apparent rejection of behavioural technology (Hewett,
1988) and hence its appeal to those who feel that a values-based, normalisation-
sound approach is incompatible with controlling, behavioural techniques - a
conflict examined by Emerson and McGill (1989). Is this reputation merited?

Gentle Teaching: what is it?

Gentle Teaching is a values-based approach to behavioural difficulties which aims to reteach the learning disabled person the importance of being with other people (human presence), being involved in activities with them (participation), and being valued as an equal by them (reward). By focusing on these three major elements McGee *et al.* assert that a mutual bond, or 'interactional equity', will be achieved, where each member of the teaching/learning process is 'empowered' but neither controls the other.

The process by which this is achieved relies on the rejection of anything that could be construed as punitive - from physical punishment using electrical shocks, through isolation, time-out procedures and over-correction to simply saying "no". The inappropriate behaviour is ignored, in the sense that it has no punitive consequence. However, it is only the behaviour and not the individual that is ignored. The inappropriate behaviour is thus given less weight in the interaction. Its function as a disruptive influence is defused.

The individual is then redirected to another activity, which ideally should be a structured part of the ordinary daily routine. This refocussing of attention can be to an apparently trivial activity, but the important element is that this activity then becomes the vehicle for the introduction of reward. The reward may appear to be non-specific, in that it has not been taken from a list of potential 'reinforcers', but McGee *et al.* argue that merely remaining with the individual signals that we value him/her as a human being, and this serves as its own reward.

Beyond the principles of 'ignore-redirect-reward' and 'interactional equity' McGee *et al.* describe a number of techniques that they have found to be of use in the teaching process. These include environmental management, stimulus control, errorless learning, shaping, fading, and assistance. All of these will be familiar to those who have studied behavioural methods. Two methods which may require some explanation are 'silent teaching' and 'reward envelopes'. Silent teaching requires that in the first instance minimal verbal instructions are used, so as to maximise the power of verbal reward. 'The value of words can easily be lost in a barrage of verbal input' (p.100). Signs, gestures and other non-verbal prompts are used instead. With the reward enveloped, enough reward is given initially so that the student learns the power of verbal and tactile praise. This is systematically and rapidly decreased, thus holding extra back in reserve so that it can be given when there is a greater need.

McGee and his colleagues acknowledge that all behaviours serve some function in our lives, and are learned because they allow us to get control over our environment. Difficult behaviours are very adaptive for some environments, although inappropriate in others. So head-banging can be seen as a logical response in a ward of non-communicating people. Its function is a basic one of communication, although it may communicate different things on different occasions.

The focus of teaching thus becomes that of teaching the replacement of behaviours, by those that are more appropriate and adaptive. 'Bonding' must be taught using these other behaviours as vehicles for teaching the value of human presence, participation and reward. Getting rid of problem behaviours before more socially acceptable ones can be taught fails to lead to bonding. The use of punishment leads to submission, and also impedes the forming of a bond.

However, more important than any technique, maintain McGee *et al.*, is the caregiver's attitude or 'posture'. This must include tolerance and affection, but goes beyond just treating the person decently. Caregivers need to look at and move away from cold, distancing and dependency-provoking attitudes, to those which accept the person as a human being, in spite of often repulsive behaviours. At the worst moments of aggression or self-injury, good caregivers remain calm, protect themselves and others, and redirect people to tasks with reward. There is no implication of pity, but rather protection of the person from harm, and a redirection towards bonding. This 'posture' is at the core of Gentle Teaching. Teaching the person, rather than changing the behaviour, is the focus. Moreover, this teaching is seen to be a process of mutual change, and therefore requires the person who takes on the role of teacher to continually question his or her values. Gentle Teaching does not preclude the use of restraint in that it does not allow people to be injured. There may be occasions when it is necessary to interrupt a behaviour to prevent harm or damage occurring. However, it is important that this does not become the preferred method of control, nor should it become punitive in nature. It should be accompanied by other, more positive types of physical contact.

Does Gentle Teaching work?

McGee *et al.* report data on 73 adults who were referred to their programme with varying levels of self-injurious behaviours. High intensity behaviours shown by 86.3% included such acts as head-banging over 1000 times per day with severe physical damage. The average length of treatment was 28 days, and a one-to-one ratio of staffing was provided for the majority for 1 to 5 days, but for 10 people it lasted between 4 and 11 weeks. All were discharged to community facilities. None displayed high intensity self injury at discharge or at follow-up, 1 to 5 years later. Just over a quarter did, however, show some signs of self injury at a low rate (fewer than 50 episodes per day) at follow-up, suggesting improvement rather than complete removal of these challenging behaviours.

Jordan, Singh and Repp (1989) were critical of the McGee work, suggesting that the results were often simply informal observations or descriptions of progress, with no accompanying baseline or other control conditions. They implied that Gentle Teaching consisted of no more than simple management techniques with a differential reinforcement procedure. Their study aimed to be more empirical, comparing the clinical effectiveness of Gentle Teaching with visual screening in the treatment of stereotyped behaviour. They also looked at the effects on other behaviours, especially social interaction with the therapist (bonding).

After establishing baseline levels of behaviour when the materials were available and simply modelled by the therapist, a 'task-training' condition was implemented, which used standard behavioural techniques of physical and verbal prompts, verbal and tactile reinforcement, and no consequences for stereotypy other than redirection to the task. Modest decreases in the stereotyped behaviours were found. Jordan *et al.* then compared baseline control conditions with Gentle Teaching, in which teaching quietly was used as the discriminative stimulus, and visual screening, where the therapist modelled to the client: 'when you do x I will do this' and covered the client's eyes with their hand, with another hand held at the back of the head.

While both procedures seemed to be more effective than the control condition, visual screening was found to be more effective in reducing stereotypy than was Gentle Teaching. 'Bonding', they say, occurred at the same low levels under both conditions. Jordan *et al.* suggest that 'the addition of an aversive procedure (i.e. visual screening)....was necessary to achieve a clinically significant effect.'

Yet did the study examine the right issues? McGee *et al.* contend that posture or attitude of the caregiver is more important than any technique, but this was not considered.

Cheseldine and Pugh (1991) recorded a reduction in severely challenging behaviours from 26% to 9% over a period of a year, in a student in a school for children with severe learning difficulties. Using the process described by McGee *et al.*, they also found an increase in appropriate behaviours from 26% to 48% over the same period. Behaviours which were described neutrally (e.g. he had yoghurt for pudding) remained approximately the same - 48% and 43%, from year one to year two.

Arguably more interesting than the changes in pupil behaviour were the staff attitudes that these authors noted. Data had been collected in the form of diaries for all the students in the class, and references to the target pupil, a boy aged 16 years, were listed and rated by staff according to whether they thought they were very negative (-2) through to very positive (+2). Staff who were perceived as being 'anti' Gentle Teaching, in the sense that it was felt that they would be likely to sabotage these teaching processes, albeit unwittingly, were found to be more likely to rate the behaviour negatively. Yet when the same statements were rated by teachers from another school, who did not know the pupil in question, this effect was not found. The teachers who were described as 'anti' Gentle Teaching were as likely to rate the behaviour positively as were Gentle Teaching's most ardent supporters. While it may be argued that the teachers who rated their colleagues according to their perceived attitude to Gentle Teaching may have not judged their respective groups in the same way, it was felt that they had worked for similar periods of time in similar settings, and that similar criteria had been used.

It seemed, therefore, that merely being opposed to the principles of Gentle Teaching, or at least unconvinced of the reasons for doing away with 'punishment', was not enough to influence one's judgement of behaviour, but that knowing the perpetrator, or at least his **reputation** for being challenging is sufficient to have an effect. These staff, who sometimes described their 'pro' Gentle Teaching colleagues as being 'soft', continued to rate behaviours more negatively in spite of documented improvements having taken place. This has serious ramifications for intervention programmes, and provides further evidence of the dangers of labelling people according to their behaviour.

Is Gentle Teaching anything new?

The debate as to whether Gentle Teaching is viewed as a method or a values system will undoubtedly continue, but are its proponents merely trying to teach grandmothers to suck eggs? It has already been noted above that some observers consider it to be no more than a collection of tried and trusted behavioural techniques (Jordan *et al.*, 1989). Similarly, Jones (1990) has described Gentle Teaching as 'behaviourism at its best'.

McGee and his colleagues contend that the unique character of Gentle Teaching lies in its emphasis on a humanizing and respectful posture towards people with severe learning difficulties, and its rejection of punishment. Normalization, or social role valorization (Wolfensberger, 1983) is well established as a process for establishing and safeguarding the rights of people with learning difficulties. La Vigna and Donellan (1986) specifically aim to identify 'normalized' approaches to managing often severe and dangerous behaviours. They describe a wide range of non-aversive behavioural techniques that can be used to this end. Gold's 'Try Another Way' (1980) stresses the need for teaching and intervention to be explicitly valuing of the client.

Gentle Teaching aims to replace inappropriate behaviours with more appropriate ones. The constructional approach (Schwartz and Goldiamond, 1975) has similar objectives, relying in part on establishing the functional importance of the 'unacceptable' behaviours. Iwata's (1982) development of experimental or 'analogue' conditions to establish such functions was a seminal paper in this respect. Similarly, Lovett (1985) repeatedly emphasises the importance of acknowledging the role of 'problem behaviours' as forms of communication, and the need to examine the social context before embarking on any sort of 'intervention'.

The quality and quantity of interactions leading to bonding have been looked at, arguably more thoroughly, in both 'normal' child development (Trevarthen, 1979) and profound mental handicap (Burford, 1990). Cheseldine and McConkey (1979) described the greater effectiveness of using non-directive methods, using principles similar to McGee's 'silent teaching' in developing the play and language of young children with Down's Syndrome. The skills-focused curriculum is already changing to the more child/client centred one, through the medium of intensive interactive teaching (Knight, see Chapter 2).

Why then is there such great interest in Gentle Teaching, to the extent that it is being welcomed as the Holy Grail? It seems rather odd that in professions typically regarded as the 'caring professions', in health and education, we should find ourselves having to examine our attitudes so closely. Perhaps it is merely a natural extension to the values system which we more readily accept and expect in other areas of the overall community care philosophy. Lovett (1985) has suggested that sometimes we become so caught up with behaviour that we forget to listen to what that behaviour is telling us. When this happens, our intervention programmes so easily slip away from being merely constructional in nature, to including an element of punishment. How many times have you heard the view that a child is deliberately doing something and should not be allowed to 'get away with it', or 'will just have to learn'? He or she then swiftly has potential reinforcers removed, through time out, or denial of treats. Yet Lovett also suggests that people usually do things to get some beneficial result, rather than merely to get themselves labelled.

We seem to have become as professionals totally behaviour-centred, or perhaps more accurately, problem-centred. How has this happened in the field of special education, while in mainstream education the focus still seems to be more on achievement and overcoming problems to do with academic attainment rather than with behaviour? A recent study by Wheldall, Houghton and Merrett (1989) in secondary school classrooms looked at teacher rates of approval and disapproval towards their pupils. In general, approval to academic behaviours was three times that for disapproval, whereas for social behaviours the reverse was true. The teachers were quick to pick up incidents of which they disapproved, yet rarely approved or commented upon desirable or appropriate social behaviours. It seemed that the teachers thought that good behaviour was no more than was to be expected, and that pupils do not need, or indeed deserve, praise or comment for conforming to the rules. However, overall there was a greater rate of approval than disapproval - more positive reinforcers than punishers. This was possible because most teacher-pupil time was task-oriented, and the pupils spent long periods of time 'on-task'. This may be the essential difference from special education.

By definition, our clients have learning difficulties, therefore they are less likely to spend time on-task, thus having fewer opportunities for approval. The remaining time is made up of largely social behaviours, of which we then become very critical. The balance of approval/disapproval rates may then be disrupted, and any positive relationship which may have existed before is soon shattered.

This is not to suggest that we should revert back to being solely task-oriented, but rather we should question our approaches and look at the balance of rewards and reinforcements that we are offering. This can be achieved through a client-centred approach.

Conclusion

Gentle Teaching may not be the quickest way to change behaviour, but it does seem to offer a variation on methods which many professionals feel to be too distancing, and which sacrifice relationships during their application. Lovett (1985) makes the point that we do not have to choose between being 'nice' and being 'therapeutic'. 'It's hard to do therapy without trust and some mutual regard, and it is equally hard to have a friendly and supportive relationship with another person that is not in some way 'good' for the people involved.' Equally, we should not become obsessed with reaching goals to the exclusion of caring how we get there. It may take longer, but our dignity, and that of clients, is more likely to be retained.

The process of Gentle Teaching undoubtedly offers an alternative to punishment for dealing with challenging behaviours, but it does not offer an alternative to a behavioural approach. Perhaps it is no more than the name itself which makes it attractive to so many. But *caveat emptor*, it is not easy. It is time consuming, in the early stages when one-to-one teaching is required, and later on, when a continued structure to the day is needed. It does not just produce a client group who will sit quietly on chairs for long periods of the day. It may be frustrating, if progress seems slow, or if colleagues say you are 'being soft'. It requires patience to practise it consistently.

The benefits may be many. Individuals are no longer excluded from the learning process. They seem to have more fun and are in control of their world in a more socially acceptable way. Special activities are needed less often for the disruptive person and they start to become part of the larger group.

Professionals often say they feel more comfortable with this approach, and many say that this is what they do anyway. The extra comfort is drawn, ironically, from the fact that is has been written about and therefore given approval for clearly defined, skill-related tasks, while socially appropriate strategies (as in the Gentle Approach) are deemed to be no more than should be expected of them! So, while we might argue grandly that Gentle Teaching represents a *rapprochement* between behavioural technology and normalisation, perhaps it will have its greatest effect by making all concerned simply feel better.

This chapter opened with a quote from Szasz that suggests that we are all out to gain credit from what we do, but usually at the expense of our client group. Gentle Teaching asks us to redress that balance.

Case study

Fiona is a 14 year old girl who lives at home with her mother, step-father, sister and two half-sisters. She attends a school for children with severe learning difficulties on a daily basis, but has from time to time been in danger of losing that place because of the aggressive nature of some of her behaviour.

Fiona's repertoire of 'inappropriate' behaviours consists of both self-injury, slapping her head, and aggression towards others - spitting, hitting, kicking, plus screaming and swearing. These behaviours generally occur when she is being requested to do something, or if she has asked for something which she has not received. All of these behaviours occur at school. At home she rules the roost, but her mother readily admits that they give in to all of her demands 'for a quiet life'. Her step-father was not prepared to become involved in any intervention programme, saying that they had found a way of coping, and did not want to rock the boat. Most of her time at home was spent sitting on the settee, demanding that others should do likewise. Her mother said that she never played, was not interested in dolls and would not allow her sisters to play with their dolls.

Fiona was in a class with six other pupils and two members of staff. The staff observed and recorded her behaviour using an antecedent-behaviour-consequence (ABC) chart, to try and establish what was causing or maintaining it. There seemed to be no regular pattern other than that the 'problems' decreased when Fiona received staff attention, and increased when the staff went to work with the other pupils.

A number of behavioural approaches had been tried, in an attempt to improve the situation. She had been given time-out from positive reinforcement, by staff turning away from her inappropriate behaviours. She had been awarded with crisps for appropriate participation. Staff had tried to redirect her to other activities, but these seemed to become either all-consuming or led to battles as she refused to participate. In general Fiona seemed a sad child, with a limited range of interests. When I first met her she started off by spitting at me across the table. I ignored this (and her), so she then came round the table and hit me. I ignored this (and her). She wandered off, came back and spoke to me. I turned to her, smiled and spoke. She hit me.

What a wonderful example of behaviour modification! Her behaviour was both functional and adaptive, in that she shaped up my behaviour so that I attended to her. My mistake was to ignore **her**, rather than just the behaviour.

Intervention has consisted of structuring her day so that there are many opportunities for her to be rewarded, and so that she might relearn the positive benefits of being near people and working with them. The flow of the day consists of play opportunities as well as the more traditional classroom tasks. There are times when she is learning to do things on her own and alongside her peer group, as well as on a one-to-one basis with staff. If she says or does something that is considered inappropriate, she is redirected to a more appropriate activity. For example, if she makes repeated demands for drinks, she is told the first time when she will have one and then staff talk about something else. In this way her conversation is acknowledged as being important, but is refocussed to other topics. The environment and setting conditions are arranged so there is little opportunity for disruption, and so that she is initially guaranteed success. Silent teaching is employed to the extent that staff try to cut down on unnecessary verbiage. To this end video recorders are invaluable. They enable us to look at **our** behaviour, and not just focus on Fiona's.

You will recall that McGee and his colleagues stress the importance of our attitude or posture. Again, video plays an important part. It enables us to go back over what we did and ask some crucial questions:

Did we provide and make use of opportunities for reward giving (i.e. showing the person how much we value them)?
What different means did we use to do this?
Were other staff and pupils involved in giving and receiving rewards/ value?
How did the pupil react to our handing out this reward?
How did we respond if the pupil initiated the sort of interaction?

It is essential that we pick up the earliest signs of this behaviour becoming reciprocal. We had a lovely scene of the pupils using a slide (shute) in the classroom, and as each pupil went up, the staff gave encouragement, and made sounds of delight as they slid down. Until it was Fiona's turn. She did the same as her peers had done, looking around for approval, but to the accompaniment of silence. How easy it is to slip into the vicious circle of expecting the challenging child not to have, or be, fun, and so not encouraging any.

The story ends (or at least continues) happily however. Fiona's disruptive behaviour has dramatically reduced so that she now never spits, and rarely hits herself or others. If she does, the staff do not reprimand her, but rather look for what she was trying to communicate. The staff say they too have changed. They say they think they understand Fiona better now, and feel more positive towards her. Fiona undoubtedly behaves more positively towards her staff and peer group. She is able to spend time with them and to have rests away from them, choosing to do other activities, rather than just sitting rocking. Now all we have to work on is the home situation.................

References

Bluma, S M, Shearer, M S, Frohmen, A H and Hilliard, J M (1976). *The Portage Guide to Early Education.* Cooperative Education Services Agency.

Blunden, R and Allen, D (eds). (1987). *Facing the Challenge.* King's Fund Centre.

Burford, B (1990). *Children with Profound Handicaps: How carers can communicate through movement.* Health Promotion Research Trust, Cambridge.

Cheseldine, S E and McConkey, R (1979). Parental speech to Down's Syndrome children: an intervention study. *American Journal of Mental Deficiency*, 83 pp 612-620.

Cheseldine, S E and Pugh, A (1991). *Gentle Teaching: state of the art or a state of mind?* Submitted for publication.

Emerson, E and McGill, P (1989). Normalization and applied behaviour analysis: values and technology in services for people with learning difficulties. *Behavioural Psychotherapy*, 17.

Foxen, T & McBrien, J (1981). *The EDY Inservice Course for Mental Handicap Practitioners.* Manchester University Press.

Gold, M W (1980). *Try Another Way: Training Manual.* Research Press.

Hewett, D (1988). Review of McGee *et al.* (op. cit.). In *Journal of British Music Therapy*, 2.

Iwata, B A, Dorsey, M F, Slifer, K J, Bauman, K E and Richman, G S (1982). Toward a functional analysis of self-injury. *Analysis and Intervention in Developmental Disabilities*, 2.

Jones, R (1990). Gentle Teaching: Behaviourism at its best? *Community Living*, 3.

Jordan, J, Singh, N N and Repp, A C (1989). An evaluation of gentle teaching and facial screening in the reduction of stereotypy. *Journal of Applied Behaviour Analysis*, 22.

La Vigna, G W and Donellan, A M (1986). *Alternatives to Punishment: Solving Behaviour Problems with Non-aversive Strategies.* Irvington.

Lovett, H (1985). *Cognitive Counselling and Persons with Special Needs.* **Praeger.**

McGee, J J, Menolascino, F J, Hobbs, D C and Menousek, P E (1987). *Gentle Teaching: a nonaversive approach for helping persons with mental retardation.* Human Sciences Press.

Mulick, J A (1990). The ideology and science of punishment in mental retardation *American Journal of Mental Retardation,* 95.

Schwartz, A and Goldiamond, I (1975). *Social Casework: the Behavioural Approach.* Columbia University.

Szasz, T S (1973). *The Second Sin.* Routledge & Kegan Paul.

Trevarthen, C (1979). Communication and cooperation in early infancy. In Bullowa, M (ed). *Before Speech: the beginnings of interpersonal communication.* Cambridge University Press.

Wheldall, K, Houghton, S and Merrett, F (1989). Natural rates of approval and disapproval in British secondary school classrooms . *British Journal of Educational Psychology,* 59.

Wolfensberger, W (1983). Social role valorization: a proposed new term for the principle of normalization. *Mental Retardation,* 21.

Learning a Sense of Self-Worth in the Face of Stigma

Andrew Jahoda

Introduction

There is increasing concern with developing a person centred approach in services for people with learning difficulties, and to counteract the stigma which these individuals face (Wolfensberger and Thomas, 1981). It is therefore surprising how little has been done to explore the feelings and experience of consumers of these services. Perhaps the problem lies in the tendency to regard people as being subject to social forces which shape their lives and self-images. The belief that people with learning difficulties are socially malleable and passive is reinforced by the commonly held assumption that they lack insight into their social situation.

There are a number of theories as to the nature and development of the self-concept. The social constructionist approach as outlined by George Herbert Mead (1934), suggested the self-concept is formed on the basis of how one is seen by significant others. For example, parents or teachers might play a particularly important role in determining the nature of a person's self-concept. Mead also attached importance to internalising societal norms and values, or the view of the 'generalised other', which enabled the person to determine her perception of self relative to the wider social world. Therefore if a person with a learning difficulty leads a segregated life in a 'handicapped' alcove of society, and is treated in a stigmatised fashion, then she is likely to internalise a stigmatised identity. However, alternative theories put forward by those such as Markova (1987) reject the view that the self is largely a product of social circumstances. She asserts that the person is an agent and may consequently develop an individual perspective of self on the basis of experience with the world.

> In becoming human, one is working to become human, indeed one has to struggle for it, as Hegel made clear. Everything a human being achieves comes from active practical involvement rather than from sheer acceptance of information and attitudes (Markova, 1987).

The fact that Markova also highlights feelings allows the prediction, on the basis of her writings, that a person might reject the negative connotations of handicap.

This chapter will set out to challenge the idea that the self-concepts of people with learning difficulties are simply moulded by social forces. After briefly outlining previous work on the self-concept, data will be drawn from a study of adults with mild learning difficulties (Jahoda, 1988) to illustrate the active role they play in determining their own view of self. Finally, the educational implications of these findings will be considered.

School studies

The vast majority of the literature concerning the self-concepts of people with learning difficulties has examined the consequences of integrated or segregated schooling. One argument is that being set apart from non-handicapped peers in a special school or class, and being formally labelled as having learning difficulties, can result in a sense of failure, rejection and an acute awareness of one's stigmatised status. The opposing outlook is that a sense of failure and rejection is more likely to be generated in a mainstream setting, because in ordinary classes the children would compare themselves unfavourably with their non-handicapped peers and possibly experience name calling and other forms of victimisation. Unfortunately a great deal of the research evidence is contradictory, and fails to weigh the balance on one side of the argument or the other.

Standardised self-concept tests

The first review of the literature (Schurr *et al.*, 1970) concluded that the lack of direction provided by the studies was due to the inadequacies of the self-concept measures which were used. The reviewers felt these measures reflected the 'thinking and biases of the researchers rather than the natural cognitions and concerns of the subjects'. For example, the Piers and Harris test (1964) consists of a collection of children's statements, covering a range of feelings and thoughts, which the researchers had standardised for all children. But how do we know that the items in the test have the same salience and meaning for children with learning difficulties as they have for other children? Indeed a recent review by Crocker and Major (1989) has argued that stigmatised people play down their stigmatised characteristics and positively emphasise other aspects of their self-concepts. This suggests that even if children have a poorer sense of self with regard to items such as intellectual ability, it does not necessarily mean they have a globally negative self-concept. Consequently, it is questionable what insight these self-concept tests can provide into the unique experience and history of any identifiable group of children, including those with learning difficulties. No matter what statistical wizardry the researcher conjures up, a decontextualised numerical score without meaning remains just that.

Social comparison

The main strand of self-concept research in special education has been based on social comparison theory. In other words, the children develop a view of self relative to a particular social group. It is suggested that children with learning difficulties do not actively choose the children with whom they are going to compare themselves. Instead they simply compare themselves with fellow pupils with whom they are in closest 'proximity' (Crocker *et al.*, 1989). Hence a special school child in a mainstream class would compare herself with her peers there. The result of this comparison would be unfavourable, and lead to lowered self-concept. In contrast, the child in a special school would compare herself favourably with fellow pupils and boost her self-concept. When taken at face value, these studies appear to support the predictions of social comparison theory. But the findings may be open to reinterpretation. For example, when Schurr *et al.* (1972) found that children's academic self-concept increased as a result of moving from mainstream to special schooling, this was not necessarily through a process of social comparison. It could equally have been the case that the children were responding to the feedback they had received from their teachers. This is because the mainstream class teachers would tend to regard these children as relatively incompetent, while in a special class these children would be seen as relatively competent.

Being school based research, the social comparison studies fail to take account of the children's awareness of self in relation to a wider social sphere. The narrow focus of the social comparison work was highlighted by a study by Rheinberg and Enstrup (1977), who found that as a group of special needs children reached the end of their school career their academic self-concept went down. Casparis (1978) interpreted this to mean that the children were becoming more aware of their poorer competence relative to non-handicapped young people with whom they would soon be in direct competition as school leavers. However, it is unlikely that the children suddenly became aware that others in the wider community were brighter than themselves.

The above, and more recent work (Bear *et al.*, 1991), is based on the premise that school reference groups have a powerful influence in determining children's self-concepts. Instead, it could be argued that the evidence shows the active part children play in constructing their own self-concepts. In doing so, they take into account the wider social consequences of special schooling, outside the hours of 9 o'clock to 4 o'clock. These children are not like ethnic minorities who may draw strength from their distinct cultural background. Instead they may have to go home and face taunts from neighbouring children, some of whom might even have been friends in the past (Cheston, 1988).

Coping with stigma

Qualitative approaches have also been used to examine the self-concepts of people with learning difficulties. Robert Edgerton, who introduced the participant observational approach to studying the lives of people with learning difficulties, carried out a classic study of people who had been discharged from a long-stay hospital (Edgerton, 1967). Using an analytical framework provided by Goffman's (1963) 'Stigma', he described how people attempted to 'deny' their handicaps and pass as 'normal'. However, Edgerton's study was in reality more concerned with the discharged patient's attempts to cope with stigma, than its consequences for their self-concepts. Case study material (Flynn 1986) and surveys (Jones 1972) have also powerfully demonstrated the effect of stigma on the lives of adults and children with learning difficulties.

Stigma and the self-concept

I will use our research (Jahoda 1988, Jahoda *et al.* 1989, Jahoda *et al.* 1990) in order to illustrate in more detail the consequences of stigma on the self-concepts of people with learning difficulties. The study examined the part which the social environment and attitudes of others played in determining the self-concepts of people with learning difficulties. The following three groups participated in the study: i) the Family group consisted of adults attending an Adult Training Centre and living at home with family members. They were selected on the basis of a survey of people attending Adult Training Centres who were considered by the management to have the potential to live semi-independently with limited staff support. As the survey included over half of those attending Adult Training Centres in one region in Scotland, the findings can be taken as quite representative. ii) The Hospital group were drawn from a wave of residents who were about to leave a long-stay hospital to live in community based residences. iii) The Housing Association group were people who had recently left their family home to live more independently in Housing Association hostels or Sheltered housing complexes. Along with participant observation, the main methods used in the study were semi-structured interviews. The interviewer did not use the words 'handicapped' or 'learning difficulty', nor imply that the participants felt stigmatised in any way. Instead, he explored their experience and raised issues thought to be pertinent to the participants' view of themselves. The participants' staff members and, wherever possible, mothers were also interviewed.

Experience of stigma

Before going on to examine the effects of stigma on the self-concepts of the participants in the research, one must begin by considering the participants' experience of stigma. After all, if the participants did not report facing stigma then this might; i) be due to their denial of handicap and the consequent stigma, ii) because they lacked the social sensitivity to be aware of it, or iii) because they did not in fact face stigma in their lives. The Family group will be used to illustrate the participants' experience of stigma, as they represented the widest population.

All twenty Family participants reported receiving stigmatised treatment of one kind or another. School attendance had a particular salience for them because it was at this stage that they had been officially labelled as 'mentally handicapped'. The realisation that they had been given such a status came sharply into focus for some when they were moved from ordinary to special schools. Others who started out in special schools, said they grasped their situation when they became aware that they went to a different school from non-handicapped siblings and peers in the neighbourhood. Indeed the participants felt that the stigma which had begun to affect their lives as children, such as being called names, being set apart from their non-handicapped peers and being unable to escape from their child-like status continued into their adult lives. This awareness was often heightened by watching brothers and sisters get jobs, get married and leave home.

The continued sensitivity towards child-like treatment was evident in the participants' complaints about Adult Training Centre staff's authoritarian attitudes. One woman explained how she felt about having to ask if she could go to the toilet:

> I feel rotten about that sometimes. The staff treat you like a school bairn when you're not even at school.

What is common to all stigmatised treatment, whether it is getting a yellow bus to a special school, being rejected and called names by non-handicapped peers in the neighbourhood, or being over-restricted by parents, is that people with learning difficulties are set apart and given an inferior social status. The participants in the study appeared to be acutely aware of stigma which pervaded almost every area of their lives, - school, family, work and their social lives and networks.

The self-concept

In the qualitative analysis the participants from the three groups were categorised into two types. Table 1 shows the distribution of participants who were categorised as essentially the same and essentially different from non-handicapped others. A finer grained analysis produced sub-categories of the participants in these broad types.

Table 1.

The number of Family, Hospital and Housing Association participants who saw themselves as essentially different or essentially the same as non-handicapped others.

	Family participants' self-concepts	Housing Association participants' self-concepts	Hospital participants' self-concepts
Essentially different	3	3	2
Essentially the same	17	7	16
Total	20	10	18

Family participants' self-concepts

In addition to the above experience of stigma, there was evidence from the study that the participants led an isolated existence, with their social lives tending to revolve around family and specially organised activities for the 'mentally handicapped'. Moreover, eight out of twelve of a sub-sample of participants' mothers considered their offspring to be 'globally' handicapped. In other words, they did not regard their offspring as having specific disabilities, but saw them as completely 'handicapped' as persons. One mother even commented that her daughter was cut off 'in her own wee world'. However, despite their social status as being 'handicapped', and many of them being treated as such by their mothers, seventeen out of the twenty participants (Table 1) rejected a stigmatised view of self and saw themselves as essentially the same as non-handicapped others. A possible explanation for the lack of impact of mothers' attitudes might have been that such attitudes did not reflect the mothers actual treatment of their son or daughter. But in fact the mothers' views did tangibly affect the participants' lives, in so far as those who were viewed as globally handicapped were afforded the least autonomy.

Contrary to the social constructionist view of self (Mead 1934), it would therefore appear that these participants' self-concepts were not simply moulded by the views of parents, staff or their prescribed social status as 'handicapped' members of society. Indeed, given the participants' social isolation, one could have predicted that the parental treatment would have had particular influence over their view of self. But retaining a positive sense of self-hood in the face of such

E

circumstances weighed heavily on many of the Family participants. Feelings of helplessness and frustration at their inability to alter their circumstances or change others' attitudes towards them, were just two of the emotions expressed. Detailing one such participant's perception of self may provide some insight into such feelings.

One sub-group of Family participants, who saw themselves as essentially the same as non-handicapped others, were termed *progressors*. They rejected the stigma against people with a learning difficulty as one would expect a marginal group in society to do. However, they also hoped for a change in their circumstances that would allow them to lead more ordinary lives. Clare was one such person.

Clare explained that the reason she went to a special school was because of her learning difficulty. However, she felt that going there had sentenced her to an educational and social backwater from which she had never managed to emerge. She felt, as she put it, that she had never been given a 'chance' and had learned 'damn all' at the special school. Referring to people working outside the Adult Training Centre Clare said:

> ..... they all went to a perfect normal school, you went to a thick stupid school.

She felt her rejection by non-handicapped others had continued since she left school. There was a sense of helplessness in Clare's comments. She was in no doubt she shared the same rights as non-handicapped people but appeared to feel that the forces which had resulted in her being a recipient of 'handicapped' services, and a stigmatised person, were out of her control. Therefore, she felt it would take a drastic change in circumstances for her situation to change. This point was highlighted in her answer to the question as to whether there was anything about herself she would like to change. She said:

> My sex for one ... I hate being a lassie. What else can I change? My brain? Get a better brain..... I can be clever.

If she could she would like to get 'right away' to somewhere like Australia, where she would like to live

> just a normal life, a normal kind of life, settle down.

Hospital participants' self-concepts

Perhaps most striking were the findings of the Hospital participants', sixteen out of eighteen of whom (Table 1) rejected a stigmatised identity. This is remarkable when one considers that eleven of them had spent the major part of their lives in institutional care, relatively cut off from what the participants themselves described as the 'outside' world. Indeed, it may have been partly through the sub-culture of the hospital that the participants were given the common language and strength to reject unfair and dehumanising practices. As one man commented:

> Well when I came in here at first, I didn't ken I was called a patient. I was always wondering what a patient was at all. I know now, I'm a patient. I thought patients were in a hospital lying in a bed. I mean I never kenned of a place called xxxx. In this hospital you're classed as patients, residents, high-grades, low-grades and all this. I never kenned I was a patient. I thought how you was to get treated just the same as anybody else outside. It should all be stopped - classed as patients ... we're no dogs or animals or that. We're just the same as anybody else. They should stop all this.

As the above quote also demonstrates, the participants did not merely reflect on their treatment in terms of the isolated world of the hospital. Instead, participants often had quite a sophisticated view of the hospital and the effect which it had on their lives. In other words they were aware of the position of the hospital in the wider social environment, and how hospital practices differed from what one would expect in the outside world.

Housing association participants' self-concepts

The Housing Association results followed the same pattern as the above groups, with seven out of the ten participants (Table 1) rejecting a stigmatised identity. A number of these participants gave optimistic accounts of how they had managed to reaffirm a positive view of their own agency when they achieved greater independence. The case material of one participant, Gavin, illustrates this point very well.

Gavin considered that he had a disability, but it was its social consequences that he found problematic. He felt that the attitudes of others towards his handicap had led to a life of overprotection and created an artificial barrier between himself and non-handicapped people. His move to a housing association hostel and the resultant sense of independence and worth had served to confirm his view of self. When he talked of friendship, he expressed most clearly his feelings about the consequences of being regarded as 'handicapped':

> Even with my pals, I never got a real pal in my life. There's fellows I knew at school, that's all they are, but they were never my pals, they wouldnae mix with me. Put it bluntly, I was never good enough for them. I use to say, - well, if I'm no good enough for them, that's it finished.

He explained that he had always found it hurtful being cossetted and had never accepted the underlying implication that he was a vulnerable individual with limited ability to reach his own decisions. He made this point when he described the discussion he had had with his brother about moving to a hostel:

> It's no you that's making my mind up for me, I'm making my own mind up for me. I'm making my mind up myself, just the same as everybody else, I only take epileptic fits but I've got a mind of my own.

Indeed, Gavin gave examples of instances where he had asserted his rights. For example, he had cashed his own pension book despite the scepticism of the post office employee. He considered that his move to the housing association had vindicated the position he had adopted all these years. With support he felt he could demonstrate his independence and worth. He described with pride how he used the train for the first time to visit his sister in Glasgow. He questioned why people in the past had worried so much about him, explaining, 'now if I'm no worried, I don't know what they were worrying about'.

Educational implications

Thinking and feeling beings. The above study indicated that people do not merely internalise the attitudes of others, but play an active part in developing a concept of self. Although often isolated, the participants appeared to have a quite sophisticated social knowledge and awareness of their position in wider society. As a result, they were sensitive to prejudicial and stigmatising treatment.. However, this sensitivity may often be masked by an outward acceptance of their social circumstances. Often a sense of powerlessness underlies such an apparent acceptance, which may mask anger, frustration and hurt. It is therefore unwise to take such acceptance at face value.

The wider social awareness mentioned above can have important implications for the education of children with special needs. For example, in a classroom setting where the emphasis may be on learning or achieving particular goals, there is a tendency to focus primarily on the level of formal cognitive functioning. Under these circumstances, the social understanding of which these children are capable has little chance of becoming manifest. A study carried out by Hughes *et al.* (1987), showed how children with severe learning difficulties, brought up in a long-stay hospital, were able to acquire quite sophisticated social knowledge from the limited sources available to them. As Hughes concluded:

> The puzzling thing for an observer is perhaps not so much that these adolescents know so little, but that a few of them with age come to know surprisingly much.

If the social awareness of these young people is more advanced than their cognitive functioning would indicate, then it is desirable that teachers and schools are aware of this in their treatment of these children. For example, the status of ordinary pupils moving through secondary education evolves as they progress through the school and into their late teens. However, young people with special needs may never be afforded such an opportunity for development and remain largely in a child-like position. How must it feel to be a teenager with special needs who spends part of the week learning skills like shopping and travelling by train, to encourage independence, and the rest of the week in a school with the doors locked in order to prevent younger or less able pupils running out?

Not only does such treatment affect the young person directly, but it is also likely to send messages to parents and influence them in the direction of limiting the autonomy afforded at home. Zetlin and Turner (1985) have pointed to the powerful influences of parental child rearing practices on the adjustment of teenagers with special needs. But teachers cannot take sole responsibility for a child's wider social and emotional life, and it is therefore desirable to have close contacts with parents and relevant bodies outside the school. For example, a teacher might wish to encourage a young person's self-confidence and enable him to have a fuller social life. In order to do this, the teacher might concentrate on skills for independent travel and shopping. However, this would be to little purpose if the young person was not allowed to leave his family home unaccompanied and had few, if any, friends to go out with or to visit. To overcome this problem it would be necessary to work on the parents, to persuade them of their son's ability to travel unaccompanied. Moreover, a volunteer bureau might help to suggest social activities which he would enjoy. Of course, it would be entirely wrong to suggest that flow of information and influence would only be one way. Teachers may have much to learn about the competencies and sensitivities of the children they work with, from parents.

Positive acceptance or active listening. Challenging behaviour is the focus of increasing concern in the field of learning difficulties. As the term suggests, the emphasis is on the challenge the person is posing to a service or staff group, and with finding the meaning or cause of that challenge. Yet how often do professionals stop to think about the emotional challenges being made on people with learning difficulties?

In psychiatry the threat to the mental health of people with learning difficulties caused by stigma (Judge, 1983) is being taken increasingly seriously. Reis and Benson (1984) pointed to 'labelling, rejection and ridicule, segregation, infantilisation, social disruption, restricted opportunities and victimisation' as causing serious problems. Hence, they felt that many of the emotional problems of people with learning difficulties would be manifest in any population subject to the same experiences. Yet in common with others, schools will rarely acknowledge, let alone address these issues. How often do teachers talk with children about name calling or their sense of isolation?

Talking with children and listening to their feelings about name calling and other stigmatised treatment is a delicate matter. But if teachers really want to help their children, then talking would make a valuable contribution. With reference to his work on school leavers, Cheston (1988) suggested that where necessary the children should be helped to develop accounts of their difficulties which do not threaten their identities. In other words, they should not blame themselves for their learning difficulties or believe that they are globally 'handicapped', and therefore completely different from non-handicapped others. On the other hand, Szivos and Travers (1988) have suggested that facilitating group discussion can help people with learning difficulties to realise that they share many of the same problems and feelings. They argue that the group identity generated by such an approach can promote self-acceptance. At the same time being part of a group must also have a positive focus and aim to solve problems, as well as to share and explore them. Whether through group or individual work, it is an issue which needs to be addressed. Teachers may feel uncomfortable with tackling this emotional and difficult subject. However, it pervades much of the children's lives and infuses their struggle to retain a positive view of self with a great deal of inner tension and conflict. Feelings of hurt, frustration and anger may be churning beneath an apparently calm and contented surface.

Integration versus segregation. If the aim of educating children with special needs is to provide them with the skills to lead active and full lives, then education has failed if these children leave school feeling alienated from their non-handicapped peers and pushed to the margins of society. Consequently, it is worth serious consideration in the educational sphere how people with learning difficulties view themselves and their relative position in society.

A number of the participants in our research had attended special school units within ordinary schools. However, this did not mean they had enjoyed wider social networks. Being set apart in an easily identifiable special needs section does not promote the acceptance of children with learning difficulties, nor does it mean children necessarily avoid name calling (Cheston, 1989). The more segregated special schools cannot save the children from bearing the social and psychological consequences of labelling. It does not provide them with a safe haven when they go home from school and have no one to play with, nor when they leave school and seek employment in competition with their peers from mainstream education. Even going straight to an Adult Training Centre did not mean that the participants in the study were sheltered from the social consequences of their disability. As one man explained his feelings about people knowing where he went to work:

They see you going to a place like that (the ATC) and they see the buses. They make a fool of you when you go out on the buses. It really gets up my nose. It's no our fault we're like that. I didn't ask to be the way I am, it's just one of those things you've got to live with. You try to talk to someone and tell them where you work, they've no time for you. Makes me feel that size, as though I could just crawl into a hole and curl up.

While the evidence would contradict the view that special schooling provides a protective environment, integrated schooling has no simple remedy for boosting people's self concepts. Integrated education cannot guarantee friendships or mutually enjoyable relationships with non-handicapped others. Indeed, teasing can make school a very dark and threatening place to be (Cheston, 1988). However, it is in the hands of the educators to work against the prejudice and name calling, and attempt to provide mutually enjoyable activities which bring children together, with or without learning difficulties.

I have been involved in a group organising holidays for young people with and without learning difficulties. The emphasis on the shared nature of these holidays has resulted in many friendships developing, which have continued outside the holiday period. There are many areas of common interest and talent which might draw children with and without learning difficulties together, such as sport, drama, music and art. Of course it might simply be that two people like each other. But without the opportunity to meet and mix, in an atmosphere which encourages mutual respect, the potential for friendship will not arise.

Adult Education. As our study was carried out with adults, perhaps the findings are particularly relevant to adult education. Participants did talk about adult education, and in particular colleges of further education. Colleges were viewed favourably by the individuals who attended them because they ascribed an adult status and were institutions which were valued by the wider population. As one person described why he would rather go to college than an Adult Training Centre:

'Cause you're going to learn skills and all that. I ken I learn skills in here, but I'd rather go to college and learn skills there ... *It makes you feel like everyone else going to college - quite good.*

The participants often felt themselves to have specific learning difficulties with essential skills such as reading and writing. Consequently it was interesting that a lecturer from the college attended by a number of the participants commented that many of his students were particularly keen on learning the traditional subjects of reading and writing. Cheston (1988) in his work on school leavers, described how one individual had expressed the belief that most of his problems were due to a lack of literacy skills. He hoped that his difficulty would be overcome through a college course. Perhaps such views were not merely evidence of people's wish to lead more ordinary lives, but related to a concern to obtain competencies which might allow them to shed their stigmatised identity.

There is increasing awareness of the issue of stigma in the lives of further education students. In the excellent anthology of poetry and short stories edited by Dorothy Atkinson and Fiona Williams (1990), entitled "Know me as I am", many contributions were based on work carried out at colleges of further education. An attempt should be made to acknowledge the collective experience of people with learning difficulties, and the strength which can be drawn from this. The stigma they face must be counteracted as much as possible while opportunities for integration are simultaneously promoted.

Conclusion

Stigma has a considerable impact on the lives of people with learning difficulties. However, being treated in a stigmatised fashion does not necessarily mean that they will internalise such a view of self. Instead, a wider social awareness may allow people with learning difficulties to differentiate between treatment which is justified by their actual handicap, and prejudice and discrimination. But being able to preserve a sense of self-worth by rejecting stigmatised treatment, does not cushion people from the emotional trauma caused by such treatment. Consequently, in the person centred approach which many services claim to adopt, there is a need to take feelings seriously and to be more conscious of the hurt which stigma causes. A group from the St Clair Centre in Fife wrote a poem about their experience of stigma for 'Know me as I am'. It was entitled 'Tell them the truth'.

> There goes the mongol up the street
> Getting on the loonybus
> The schoolbairns call
> Making faces at us
> Calling us names
> Headcase, spassy, wally
> Nutter, Dylan, Twit!

> There goes the dumb-bell into the nut house!
> The schoolbairns are all daft themselves
> They should see a psychiatrist
> About their brains
> It makes you mad, it boils up your blood
> Their wooden heads are full of nonsense

> They've got nothing else to do
> Except make fun of us
> We are human beings
> And should be treated as equals
> Treated as adults
> Tell them the truth.

Written by Donald Lack, Robert Drysdale, Margaret Williamson, Derek Mustard, J.R Grubb, Joan Cargill and Robert McMahon.

References

Atkinson, D and Williams, F (Eds). (1990). *Know me as I am: an anthology of prose, poetry and art by people with learning difficulties.* Hodder and Stoughton.

Bear, G G, Clever, A and Proctor, W A (1991). Self-perceptions of non-handicapped children and children with learning difficulties in integrated classes. *The Journal of Special Education*, 24.

Casparis, J (1978). Personlichkeitsmerkale unter dem Einzlub von Etikettierungs- und Bezaugsgruppeneffekten: Ein Reinterpretation. *Zeitschrift f Entwicklungs psychologie u Padagogische Psychologie*, X.

Cheston, R (1988). *Special Education Leavers in Central Scotland: A Socio-Psychological Perspective.* Unpublished PhD Thesis, University of Stirling.

Crocker, J and Major, B (1989). Social Stigma and Self-esteem: The Self-Protective Properties of Stigma. *Psychological Review*, 96.

Edgerton, R B (1967). *The Cloak of Competence.* University of California Press.

Flynn, M C and Knussen, C (1986). What it means to be labelled 'Mentally handicapped'. *Social Work Today*, 17.

Goffman, E (1963). *Stigma: Notes on the management of spoiled identity.* Prentice-Hall.

Hughes, D, May, D and Harding, S (1987). Growing up on Ward Twenty: the everyday life of teenagers in a mental handicap hospital. *Sociology of Health and Illness*, 9

Jahoda, A (1988). *Experience of stigma and the self-concept of people with a mild mental handicap.* Unpublished PhD thesis, University of Stirling.

Jahoda, A, Markova, I and Cattermole, C (1988). Stigma and the self-concept of people with a mild mental handicap. *Journal of Mental Deficiency Research*, 32.

Jahoda, A, Cattermole, M and Markova, I (1990). Moving out: an opportunity for friendship and broadening social horizons? *Journal of Mental Deficiency Research*, 34.

Jones, R L (1971). Labels and stigma in special education. *Exceptional Children*, 38.

Judge, C (1983). The self-awareness of mentally retarded persons. *Psychiatric Aspects of Mental Retardation Newsletter*, 2.

Mead, G H (1934). *Mind, Self and Society*. University of Chicago Press.

Markova, I (1987). *Human Awareness*. Hutchinson Educational.

Piers, V E and Harris, D B (1964). Age and other correlates of self-concept in children. *Journal of Educational Psychology*, 55.

Reis, S and Benson, B A (1984). Awareness of negative social conditions among mentally retarded, emotionally disturbed outpatients. *American Journal of Psychiatry*, 141.

Rheinberg, F and Enstrup, B (1977). Selbstkonzept der Begabung bei Normal - und Sonderschulern gleicher Intelligenz: Ein Bezugsgruppenefekt. *Zeitschrift f. Entwicklungspsychologie u Padagogische Psychologie*, IX.

Schurr, K T, Joiner, L M and Towne, R C (1970). Self-concept research on the mentally retarded: a review of empirical studies. *Mental Retardation*, 8.

Schurr, K T, Towne, R C and Joiner, L M (1972). Trends in self-concept of ability over 2 years of special class placement. *Journal of Special Education*, 6.

Szivos, S E and Travers, E (1988). Conciousness Raising among Mentally Handicapped People: A Critique of the Implications of Normalisation. *Human Relations*, 41.

Wolfensberger, W and Thomas, S (1981). The principle of normalisation in human services: A brief overview. In Lisham, J (ed), *Research Highlights Number Two: Normalisation*. Aberdeen People's Press.

Zetlin, A L, Heriot, M J and Turner, J L (1985). Self-concept measurement in mentally retarded adults: A micro-analysis of responses, *Applied Research in Mental Retardation*, 6.

Early Education for Under Three Year Olds with Multiple Impairments

Catriona Dairon

Introduction

Westerlea is a day school in Edinburgh, run by the Scottish Council for Spastics, which caters for around sixty severe and profound multiply handicapped children. The majority of pupils have cerebral palsy, but in recent years some pupils have been diagnosed as having syndromes or metabolic abnormalities which produce a range of disorders similar to those of a child with cerebral palsy.

In addition to profound mental and physical handicaps, many children also have severe sensory impairments. The pupils are amongst the most dependent in the community. Indeed, prior to the Education (Scotland) Act 1974, which stated that all children should receive an education, such children would have received 'care and therapy'. The school now provides an environment in which each child is offered opportunities to develop his full potential, no matter how limited this may be in any area. Children attending the school are aged between three years and eighteen years. The majority are from Lothian Region, but some travel daily from Central, Fife and Tayside. There is a large staff which includes highly trained and qualified teachers, physiotherapists, speech therapists, occupational therapists and classroom assistants. The school also has two school nurses, an educational psychologist and a social worker. Volunteers also assist on a regular basis.

Recent developments at the school include the provision of a post-school placement for students aged eighteen to twenty-five years. This resource acknowledges the need for continuing emphasis on the development of life skills and recognises the importance of continuing therapy input to school leavers. With limited appropriate placings available for many of our school leavers, this project is a much valued resource.

The other major development in recent years has been the establishment of the Early Education Centre for children aged below the age of three, and their parents/carers. The following chapter will describe the setting up of this Centre, the philosophy on which the curriculum is based, implementation of the approach used, and finally an evaluation of this approach.

The Early Education Centre

The Scottish Council for Spastics has long recognised the need for therapy input from an early age, and physiotherapy and occupational therapy has been provided by the external therapy services for many years. Local Authorities have provided pre-school educational services, and Health Board and Social Work staff also offer both practical and emotional support to handicapped children and their families.

However, from comments of parents of children entering the reception class at school, it was apparent that children and families could sometimes be overwhelmed by the input of a range of professionals who 'told' them what to do or what not to do. Often the advice or information was contradictory or confusing and left the parent confused and feeling totally inadequate. On the other hand, other families seemed to receive very little input or contact from professionals, some receiving only physiotherapy. It was often such parents who said "I wish I'd known about this before now. I could have been working in this way with my child over the last year".

It was clear that parents required a number of things. The first was a co-ordinated approach from the professionals involved. They also wished for information to help their child develop in all areas (eg communication and cognitive development) and they wished to be involved in contributing to their child's development. It was in direct response to parents' comments that the Scottish Council agreed to some additional input to pre-school children to address this gap in existing provision. A teacher and speech therapist were engaged to work with a small group of pre-school children who were already receiving physiotherapy and occupational therapy through the external therapy services. This first step was taken in October 1986. There are currently twenty three children on the roll, who attend twice weekly.

The first four children were aged between eighteen and twenty-four months and all hoped to come to Westerlea School at the age of three years. These children and their parents were offered one morning session per week. The sessions were planned by the teacher and speech therapist and the emphasis was initially very much on activities to establish basic communication systems for the children, to develop comprehension of language, and practical skills like feeding and drinking. The parents worked throughout with their child and were given advice on appropriate activities: language, how to recognise and interpret responses, and practical advice on feeding skills, so that they could apply the same approaches at home and elsewhere. It soon became apparent that regular contact was needed with the physiotherapist, for example for advice on appropriate seating for meal times and other activities. Similarly with the occupational therapist, whose advice on suitability of cups, spoons etc was also required. The need for this type of input was relayed to the Scottish Council, who once again responded positively by employing two members of the school staff - a physio - and an occupational therapist, for a few hours per month on a consultancy basis, to Early Education. The Scottish Council for Spastics was actively investigating whether or not the principles of Conductive Education could, or should be introduced into its three

Scottish Council schools. Many schools in England had been using the principles of Conductive Education with varying degrees of success for many years. Members of staff at Westerlea including myself were given an opportunity to visit some of these schools in England.

Conductive education

Most professionals who are involved with the children and families of physically disabled children will be familiar with the term 'Conductive Education'. However, there are still those who have misconceptions about what Conductive Education is.

First and foremost it is a system of education. It was developed in Hungary by Andras Peto (1893-1967). The development of this system was directly related to the system of education in Hungary, which does not allow a child to receive education in general or special schools unless he is able to walk and take part in school activities without the use of aids. He is expected to cope with stairs, use normal toilet facilities, write and in general to participate in all aspects of the school curriculum.

The system of Conductive Education was developed to produce orthofunction in children with motor disorders, to enable them to take their place and function as pupils of the Hungarian general or special school system. (Cottam & Sutton, 1986).

Andras Peto also created the profession of conductors and established the form their training should take. It lasts for four years and closely links theory and practice, and covers many aspects of child development. This equips them to be solely responsible for a child's requirements for development - physical, emotional, academic, cognitive, and thereby makes unnecessary the involvement of a range of professionals, teachers, nurses and therapists.

Philosophy of the Early Education Centre

The Early Education Centre adopts the same philosophy as the school, which aims to provide for each child to develop in areas of

1. Physical Development (Gross Motor and Fine Motor Skills)
2. Communication Skills
3. Self Help/Independence Skills
4. Social/Emotional Development.

An eclectic approach, which includes some principles of Conductive Education, has been adopted. In addition the Centre emphasises the importance of early intervention for the development of all skills. The Centre caters for children under the age of three years and no lower age limit for admission has been set. The recognition of 'parents as partners' is reflected in our approach. Staff work closely with parents on all aspects of development and parents, not staff, work with the child throughout each session. The overall focus is on emphasising the positive, and to motivate the child to become an active participant in his environment.

The decision to incorporate principles of Conductive Education into our programmes entailed some major changes in our approach. The first was that a unified approach to teaching/learning was developed.

Team approach

Peto created and developed the profession of conductor to provide a unified approach to learning. We do not have conductors on our staff but as stated earlier, the school has a large staff of specialist teachers and therapists who were already working in multi-disciplinary teams. However, this was not totally satisfactory as some staff were conscious that by just participating in some activities, they were not fully aware of how a child interacted in others. It was therefore agreed that, as far as possible, each team member would work alongside each of the other team members throughout the week and that each team member would lead a range of activities throughout the week. In this way each of the core members of the team could learn from one another and have a better understanding of the development of skills, seeing the child as a whole. This meant that planning, input, recording and evaluation was done as a team and resulted in a more unified approach to learning by occupational, speech, and physiotherapists and teachers.

Development of all skills incorporated into all activities

Although the focus at any one time may be on a specific area of development like choice making, opportunities to constantly reinforce other skills like attention span, positioning, gross motor/fine motor movement, use of language, concept formation and peer awareness are always sought. This may not be done satisfactorily when the team is in its early stages, as team members are inclined to focus on their own aspect of child development. As teams work together longer, there is no doubt that each member learns much from his colleagues and becomes more adept at spotting opportunities for extending and reinforcing a range of skills. Each also has a better understanding of a child's abilities and personality.

Emphasis on social and emotional development

One rather sad aspect of the fragmented approach to a child where, for example, the physiotherapist concentrated on improving muscle tone, the speech therapist, his chewing pattern, the occupational therapist checked that he was provided with a suitable chair and bath aid, and the teacher ensured that object/picture, making was progressing, was that little or no attention was paid to the child as a person.

Was he a happy little boy? Was he totally passive? Did he demand Mum's attention at all times? What was Dad's relationship with him? Did he accept that his sister sat on Mum's knee for a story? How did he react to strangers - to new settings and so on. The emotional and social development of the child was often neglected. We are all familiar with the child who responds only when an adult comes into view, and has come to expect attention from an adult on a one-to-one basis. This child may be in a class of other children, but rarely relates to them. We also know of the demanding child who expects one hundred percent attention from Mum whenever she appears, and the child who is totally passive, as all his needs are anticipated and met by well intentioned adults. What need is there for such a child to make any effort? Learned dependency can become established very early on.

We are social beings by nature and whether our circles of contact are small family units or extend to a range of other settings, we must learn to live, play and work with others. We feel it is important to help our children to be able to participate in social groups and contribute to social activities and relate to a range of people, again within the limits of their capabilities.

First of all the child has to feel secure emotionally, to feel loved and to have positive feelings about himself. By developing good relationships between mother and child and other family members, the foundations are laid for the fostering of other relationships. Within our groups, this is shown by the child's acceptance of team members and other Mums, and later still through interaction with them. Other children in the groups become part of their social world and over time it is lovely to observe the developing awareness and relationships between children. They learn to accept turn taking and that there are times when someone else receives attention. They become more interested in their peers and do not always rely on adults for interaction. They also learn that if they really wish to choose someone or something that they have to indicate this. Children who learn early on in this way become children who are much more acceptable socially and who can in turn benefit in many ways from being involved in social settings.

Many families in the past have been reluctant and embarrassed to go out and about with their child because of his demanding behaviour or reaction to adults and other children. This often placed severe restriction on the families' social contacts and caused stresses within families and on marriages. We hope to enable both children and parents to participate as fully as possible in the range of social activities they enjoy.

Skills taught in meaningful contexts

Peto placed great emphasis on the importance of the timetable - how the whole day and all routine activities of day to day life can be incorporated and used as meaningful learning situations. Some examples highlight how this is done in the Early Education Centre. Dressing and undressing skills are developed prior to the start of each session's movement programme when children have to get their outer clothes off and change into T-shirts and shorts. This is not a contrived situation - there is a reason for getting clothes changed. Similarly, at the end of the programme, socks, splints and boots are put on prior to walking. Walking is built into the session as a functional activity. We have two rooms in the Centre and walking practice is incorporated at the point when we go from one room to another. Feeding skills are taught at lunch time at the end to the morning session and hand washing after messy activities.

The group approach

Another major change in our approach was that all teaching should take place in the group situation, rather than on a one-to-one basis with children receiving individual therapy to treat specific disorders. Groups are limited to a maximum of ten children. It is important to state that none of our groups are homogeneous. In each group we have a wide range of ages, physical and cognitive abilities and sensory impairments. It has not been difficult to work with a wide range of physical disabilities because the parent of each child works with him. Working with a group of children with a wide range of cognitive skills, however, is very demanding. Care has to be taken to use language and music that is relevant to the profoundly handicapped child and yet stretch those that have cognitive skills that need to be developed. With children with severe sensory impairment it is important to select very carefully the materials and activities used. The recent provision of a Snoezelen (a multi-sensory environment) has helped us overcome this problem, as the more severely sensory-impaired children can spend time here where their needs can be more appropriately addressed and this enables more demanding activities to be planned for more cognitively able children.

It must also be remembered that the levels of understanding of parents vary. It is therefore important to highlight throughout each session the responses being given by the children, in order to make mums more aware of these and to handle sensitively situations that could cause distress or despondency. It is also extremely important to keep restating the reasons for doing things and how a child's responses and skills in one activity can be used in other settings. All of this requires careful planning, not only of space, equipment, materials and activities, but also a sound knowledge of each child's abilities and each Mum's concerns and level of understanding.

Parents as partners

Before a child is offered a place at the Early Education Centre, the parent or main carer is required to give an undertaking to attend with the child, and work with him/her throughout each session. Most parents are delighted to do so and enjoy being given a central role in the team, working with their own child. The child is with the parent twenty four hours per day and by sharing expertise the parent is then best placed to ensure that learning and development of all skills can continue at all times. Initially the emphasis is on developing good relationships between child and parent and to help parents understand the needs of their child. The development of a positive attitude to the child is important, as is the importance of encouraging active participation - not anticipating needs, but giving time to the child to complete a task or achieve a goal. The development of good handling skills, learning how the child communicates, developing self-help and how to encourage participation - no matter how limited - are all included in the aims for parents. They are also made aware of the importance of routine, repetition and consistency, both in handling and use of language. They learn that everyday routines and events can be used as effective teaching/learning situations and that there is no need to set aside time for a 'work' session in order to learn. Team members can also learn much about the child by listening to parents.

Giving parents a sense of worth rather than de-skilling them, as so often happens, is one of our priorities.

The use of rhythmical intention

This was the term used by Peto to refer to the way language was used when working on a task series. What is meant by this in simple terms is that the leader of the group states what the child should do (the goal) and she states it in a rhythmical way, either by repeating the important word two or three times, or by counting, for example: "I lie down - down, down - down", or "I lie down - one, two, three". After the leader states the intention the child repeats it (or the mother, if the child cannot speak) and the child then performs the movement rhythmically. The rhythmical intention has many benefits. Its main function is to provide a child with the ability, through language, to prepare for and plan a movement and then to carry it out.

Conductive Education was developed for children who would have ability to comprehend language used in this way, initially in specific task series, but then later in other situations. The relationship between language, movement and function is crucial, with the development of these strongly inter-dependent. Many of our children do not have this level of understanding. Nevertheless, the use of rhythmical intention has benefits even for children of limited ability. The language we use is kept as simple as possible, so that the child has a better chance of developing an understanding of the language used. The same language is used each time a movement, or series of movements, is performed. This consistency in use of language, the routine and the repetition are initially important for our children. There is always a direct relationship between the words used and the action taken, allowing associations to be made.

The use of rhythm gives the child time to complete a movement while the words are being spoken, or while counting. Our children need time to change positions, for example from sitting to lying, and this enables them to organise themselves and keep control of their heads, as they perform this change of position. Movement to rhythm also helps produce a more fluid movement. The repetitive use of words and movement has often encouraged children to develop some speech. Often the first words children have attempted are those which are used in rhythmical intention. It also helps develop anticipation. It is amazing how many children learn the routine of parts of the programmes and get great pleasure from demonstrating through their actions that they know what comes next.

Music

Anyone who has worked with profoundly handicapped children will be aware of how they respond to music in a different way from other sounds. A person singing can often gain attention from a child when a spoken voice will not. Those who have had the privilege of working alongside a music therapist and profoundly handicapped children cannot have failed to be amazed at the responses they manage to evoke from some children who have shown little response to other stimuli. As many of the children who attend the Early Education Centre do not have the cognitive skills to understand the language we use in rhythmical intention, we include many songs throughout the programmes. Again many professionals are surprised at the responses of some of our very severely or profoundly handicapped children who, over many months, do appear to associate the songs with some movements. It also makes the sessions more enjoyable for the other more able children, some of whom learn to sing along.

Musical instruments are also used both during movement programmes and other activities. They can be used to develop many skills - listening (for example, for very soft sounds, anticipation, for tolerating loud sounds) for development of fine motor skills, for reaching/grasping/holding/releasing, flat hands for playing, and gross arm movements. The development of concepts such as loud, soft, noisy, no noise, and development of language can take place in musical activities. Scope for development of many skills can be created through music and through play in general.

Children at play

Children at this early age learn most skills through play. Our children should be given the same opportunities. Play has been defined in many ways. The one I like best is that 'play is child's work'. Learning should be fun, it should be varied, and through providing children with a wide range of play situations and activities, skills which are practised in a structured way in the first part of the session can then be used functionally in play. Social skills, peer awareness, interaction can also be developed through play. Action songs, nursery rhymes, finger rhymes and other songs are used extensively. They are used universally by Mums and children and our children should not be denied this. Childhood is a part of life that should be valued in its own right and I feel that it would be unforgivable to deprive any child of this in our anxiety to ensure that they must learn certain skills which they will need to progress in the future: a balanced programme must be provided. In our culture play is recognised as an important way in which young children learn. In our programmes we have therefore retained opportunities to learn through play. As a result we believe that children receive an input that combines that which we know to be effective and valuable in our own education system with what is best in Conductive Education.

Active participation and motivation

Whatever the activity, the emphasis throughout is on encouraging the child to do as much as possible for himself, within the limits of his capabilities. To do this the child must be motivated. Tasks presented must be achievable, as it is through success that the child develops a positive image of self. The praise he receives for his success also helps to motivate him to strive again even when goals are made slightly more demanding. It is important that activities are interesting to the child, that he feels it worth making the effort. It is also important that ample opportunities are created for the child to practise developing skills regularly to establish them. A variety of similar activities need to be provided to maintain interest so that boredom does not set in by being asked to do the same tasks too often. The environment should be such that the child is not distracted by unnecessary attractions. This highlights the importance of preparation, by planning of the room and each day's activities in order to ensure that maximum benefit can be derived from each session.

Methods of recording progress

Methods used at present to record the progress of the children are not wholly satisfactory. Much time was spent initially scrutinising readily available assessment charts, so that regular checks could be made on specific aspects of development. However, although parts of various charts were considered useful such as the PVCS (Kiernan and Reid, 1987), none were in fact suitable for our needs. Our main difficulty, given the range of abilities of children attending, was to find a form of assessment that would record the very minute signs of progress of our most handicapped children, and that was not so bulky and unwieldy as to be too time consuming to complete or to analyse. On the other hand some of our children were functioning at an age appropriate level in some areas of development like expressive language, and yet at an early level in some other skills.

As parents are involved in our work at the Centre, we were also very conscious of the possible effect that regular filling in of charts might have on them. Written presentation of their child's abilities, particularly for the severely and profoundly handicapped children, can often appear very negative: they highlight the degree of handicap, rather than any achievements. For these, and other reasons, the main one being the lack of time available to develop our own forms of assessment, and the importance of assessment based mainly on continuing team observation, we decided on the following system:

1. As soon as possible after being admitted to the Centre, the team educational psychologist, together with the parent, fills in a PIP chart (McConkey). This is done based on the psychologist's observations of the child and information given by the parent. Right from the start an effort is made to recognise the parent's knowledge of her child and to involve her in this process.

    From this we get a profile of the child. It may not be comprehensive, but it does give an indication of what he can do in each area of development. These positives then provide the starting point on which we work and help the child to develop and build on. Occasionally, if a parent makes a request for an assessment, or before the child leaves the Centre, and if appropriate, the educational psychologist will use the Griffiths Baby Scale to make a more formal assessment.

2. Over the next weeks or months both parent and child gradually settle into the group and over this period of time each member of the team has the opportunity to observe their reactions and progress within the group. Although each team member looks for indications of progress with her own professional eye she is also alert to noting any other observations.

    Conversations with parents are also ways of receiving information about how the child is outwith the Centre. Parents are encouraged to provide this additional information as it makes a valuable contribution to the description and understanding of the child as a whole. Talks with parents also indicate how they are coping emotionally and how their attitudes may be changing. Although the educational psychologist, the social worker and the medical officer all make home visits, none of the core team are able to do so, and all are conscious that because of this our picture of the child is not complete, and is in effect based on contact within the Centre. The regular contact and parental input of information helps offset this, in a small way. Should additional time become available to team members in future, arrangements to make home visits would be a priority.

    When team members feel that they have collected sufficient

information as a result of their observations over a period of time, and discussed specific aims with parents, all this information is pooled and discussed and a few aims for the child are then highlighted. These are listed under each area of development, and the form used is the one suggested by the Jordanhill Report (Browning *et al.*, 1983). These are then discussed again with the parent and she is invited to comment on them or ask for further explanations of them if necessary. The parent is given a copy of this individual educational programme after final amendments have been made.

3.   An additional way of recording is the use of our video camera. Each group has an entire session videoed once a month. There are benefits and drawbacks associated with this type of recording. The first drawback is that, if you record for two or three hours, you then require at least that time, but in reality much more, to play it over and re-run parts in order to note some particular reaction of a mother or child. Another disadvantage is that a member of the team is needed to operate the camera each time and this affects input to that group. Initially some children and parents can be very conscious of being filmed and do not react in the usual way. It is surprising how quickly they do come to accept it as a regular occurrence, however. Enabling parents to view can also be a problem. At present the video is put on early or during coffee time in the morning session following videoing, so that parents who particularly wish to view can do so.

        The benefits of regular videoing are very real. It enables both parents and staff to remind themselves of how parents and child were when they first came to the group. Often progress on a day to day or even week to week basis is difficult to pin-point, but by being able to look back several months, it is often very reassuring and encouraging as differences are usually quite marked. Aspects of development, like attention span, which are very difficult to describe on paper, can be noted very easily on video. Parents may not always be able to see how their child reacts, his facial expression or small gesture, when working with him. Looking at the video enables staff to point out these things. Peer awareness and aspects of social development are also easier to observe and record on video. Besides providing a record of the parent and child within the group, videos can be used for teaching and reassuring parents.

        Occasionally other professionals involved with the child, on a one-to-one basis, visit to observe the child within the group, only to find Mum and child are absent. By being able to show a section of video an otherwise disappointing visit can be avoided. Videos often enable team members to note things that perhaps they had not spotted when teaching a group. Team members tend to be very self-critical and use videos as a means of self evaluation and often take steps to alter and improve their own performance as a result of watching themselves on screen.

This combination of methods is our present method of recording. We acknowledge that it is not specific enough to be totally satisfactory but given the number of children involved and the time available to us, this is the way we feel best able to resolve this very difficult problem at present.

Evaluation of methods

The Early Education Centre has been operating in its present form since April 1989, when we moved into our new premises. This means that the evaluation of this approach is based on information gained over a relatively short space of time. The comments and observations that follow are not supported by any formal scientific data. It is impossible to set up a control group to use as a basis for comparison and therefore to measure outcome. Many changes are extremely difficult to measure such as development of attention span, or of peer awareness. Those who choose to discount claims that the approaches used provide a range of beneficial outcomes are entitled to do so because of lack of concrete evidence. Claims made are based mainly on the observations of members of staff, all experienced professionals who have worked over many years in what has been described as the traditional way, with a strong emphasis on one-to-one teaching or treatment. Each member of staff is well placed to compare the development of the skills and personalities of the children as a result of previous methods and approaches currently used.

The observations noted are not based solely on those of the team at the Early Education Centre but also on reports from staff in the two reception classes in the school who are in the position of receiving children who have attended the Centre, and also those who came direct from home and have not received this type of input before. Professionals in the community who are also closely involved both with children and their families have provided valuable feedback, as have at times other members of the family, particularly regarding emotional stresses and relationships within the family and how the children have been affected. A Questionnaire to parents has also provided useful information.

Collectively these sources supplied the information on which the following claims are based:

Changes in parents

1. Their handling skills are much improved.
2. They have a better understanding of their child's needs.
3. They have a better understanding of their child's abilities and limitations.
4. They are more consistent in their handling of their child and in their use of language.
5. They appreciate the need for consistency, routine and repetition.
6. They give their child time to respond. They encourage his active participation (within the limits of his capabilities).
7. They are more aware of the importance of seeing their child as a whole and developing a range of skills.
8. They appreciate the value of play, games, songs and rhymes as a means of learning for their child.
9. They are more aware of the opportunities for learning/teaching that exist in daily routines, at home, in school and in the environment.
10. They have a better understanding of why we include the activities we use.
11. They acquire a range of skills from team members and other parents.
12. They develop more relaxed relationships with the professionals they work with.
13. They are better prepared and therefore more able to cope with their child's transfer to another provision appropriate to his needs at the age of three years or before.

Changes in children

1. They are more tolerant of physical handling.
2. They have increased awareness of 'self' (ie respond to name, better awareness of body parts and spatial awareness).
3. They are more sociable. They accept being one of a group and accept turn taking.
4. They have increased peer awareness.
5. They are more able to use group settings to learn through imitation, interaction and competition.
6. They are more able to attend to people and activities not involving themselves.
7. They demonstrate anticipation during activities and songs routinely used.
8. They are more able to make choices and express likes and dislikes.

9.   They have an increased attention span.
10.   They adapt to change more easily (for example on transfer from Early Education to school they settle very quickly).

These are mainly differences noted in the children who transfer to the school and can be compared with direct entrants.

Many other children do in fact progress to higher levels of development in a range of skills and proceed to a range of different provisions more appropriate to their needs. Many children who develop speech and are almost walking independently and who demonstrate cognitive skills that are age appropriate go to their local nursery, play group or special school. We have no information on how they present to staff compared to similar entrants who have not had this type of experience.

Conclusion

Have our approaches enabled us to achieve our stated aims? I believe that there is a close correspondence between our stated aims and observed outcomes.

The changes in our practice have been strongly influenced by Conductive Education, but also by other factors. It is this balance that I believe has enabled us to improve the quality of the education we now provide. Our approach is a blend, and incorporates many tried and tested methods from our own Scottish system of education. We have combined those benefits that are provided by using Conductive Education but also recognised where our own system offers more. For example, many advances have been made in the field of communication in our system. Alternative and augmentative forms of communication have opened up a whole world to children who cannot speak. Daily, almost, technology is producing other systems and access to them for non-speakers. Such facilities are not given recognition in Conductive Education. Similarly in other areas we see the range of adaptations on offer - eg to cups, plates, cutlery - as additional means of facilitating independence. The recognition of the importance of giving children the opportunity to learn through play in our society is also reflected in our programme. Learning must be enjoyable. No one system or any one person can provide us with the tools we need in education. It is by selecting carefully from the range of approaches available that the needs of particular children can best be met. Those of us who have been involved in developing the Early Education Centre are in no doubt that the approaches we now use are providing children with a better start in life. It is certainly a way of working that can be fraught with difficulties, demands and stresses, both physical and emotional. It is not an approach that can be developed or established overnight. However, the rewards compensate for earlier teething troubles.

Already the ever increasing number of professionals who come to visit the Centre express interest in our work and provide us with the knowledge that we are now regarded as a model from which others can develop similar provisions. Hopefully a range of resources can gradually be established throughout the country, giving more children and their families the opportunity to benefit. These professionals however, require the support of their Local Authority funding. This is not always available although in some regions the pooling of resources and sharing of costs has been agreed for some joint ventures. Because of the present system where statutory bodies like Health, Education and Social Work operate and provide funding separately, provision to young children and families is bound to be fragmented, thus creating additional problems to those they are intended to help. There is a real need for the establishment of a statutory body, jointly funded by Health, Education and Social Work, whose remit would be to address the needs of multiply handicapped children under five and their families. This could improve co-ordination of resources and facilitate the establishment of similar Early Education Centres.

Note

The Centre is funded totally by the Scottish Council for Spastics. There is no obligation on a Local Authority to pay for the educational provision of a child before the age of five years, although in many cases children, especially those with special needs, are funded from the age of three years. Despite the interest in the work of the Centre and increasing recognition from members of Health Boards, Education Authorities and Social Work Departments that this is a valuable provision of early education for young children and their parents, this has not been accompanied by tangible support in the form of contribution to the funding of the Centre. It was hoped that the amendment to the Education (Scotland) Act 1987, that a Record of Needs may now be opened from the age of two years, would in fact persuade departments to reconsider their decision. However, to date, there has not been any change in attitude and the present status of Lothian Region finances does not augur well for any immediate support.

References

Browning, M *et al.* (1983). *Identifying and meeting the needs of profoundly mentally handicapped children.* Jordanhill College of Education.

Cottam, P and Sutton, A (eds). (1986). *Conductive Education.* Croom Helm.

Kiernan, C and Reid, B (1987). *Preverbal communication schedule.* NFER -Nelson.

McConkey, R *Parent Involvement Project Developmental Charts.* Hodder and Stoughton.

Warnock Commitee (1978). *Special Educational Needs: Report of the Commitee of Enquiry into the Education of Handicapped Children and Young People.* HMSO.

Year Round Educational Provision - meeting the challenge at Oaklands School

Sue Harland

Background

Willowbrae House was a Day Care Centre for children with severe and profound learning difficulties, run by the Social Work Department in East Edinburgh. Teaching provision, introduced in the mid Seventies, had increased to six teachers and a headteacher by the mid Eighties. The teachers worked alongside care staff employed by the Social Work Department.

For some time, it had been the intention of the authorities to split the Social Work and Educational function and to establish a separate school. When this became a realistic possibility, parents became concerned that what had been a year-round care in the old establishment would now be reduced to term-time care only. Respite hostels would only be offering care associated with school placement and would not be fulfilling a total day-care function during school holidays.

The parents put their case to the authorities and after some debate, it was decided that Willowbrae House School would provide an educational service throughout holiday periods. In August 1987 the Social Work function ceased. Nursery nurses and auxiliaries were recruited by the Education Department. Thus began the 'extended school year' for Willowbrae pupils.

The changeover demanded major readjustments from all staff. In addition, the school was further unsettled by a move to new premises on the other side of the city in August 1988. At this time, it was redesignated Oaklands School.

Setting the scene

Oaklands School is set in a grassy campus in the west of Edinburgh. It is flanked by two primary schools and shares premises with the St Giles team, which provides visiting services for partially hearing children in mainstream schools. The school presently offers an educational service every week day except for 11 public holidays and 5 staff training days. At Oaklands, we aim to meet the complex special needs of children and adolescents with severe and profound learning difficulties. The roll is currently thirtysix. The pupils are organised into six classes each with a teacher and a small team of nursery nurses and classroom auxiliaries. The headteacher and assistant head have no direct class responsibilities.

The Health Board provides two full-time nurses and part-time speech therapy, occupational therapy and physiotherapy. We also have the services of a dental officer and dental hygienist. The school doctor, community paediatrician and health visitor are in school on a regular and frequent basis. The input of medical staff and therapists is crucial to both the educational and health needs of the pupils. Input is concentrated on Tuesdays and Fridays so that 'health' staff can work as a team and so that communication with 'education' staff is facilitated. As team leader for the class, the teacher co-ordinates information from therapists, parents, medical staff and education staff in drawing up and implementing an individual educational programme for each pupil. This programme is subject to ongoing assessment and to annual multidisciplinary review involving all the above groups, the Social Work Department, appropriate respite/care agencies and the educational psychologist. Each individual programme must also be couched within a meaningful curricular whole - that is, themes and activities which relate to our aims as a school. In addition there must be a cohesion and unity in the methods and approaches used both within a class team and across the school. If children are to make progress, the educational experience must be closely co-ordinated. All this presupposes a high level of interaction and communication both amongst educational staff and across professional boundaries.

To anyone from a similar educational setting, this will be a familiar scenario. I make no apology for detailing it since it illustrates the intensity of the work for educators of our children and the high level of commitment from all staff.

Although we have opted in Oaklands to create a different atmosphere in holiday periods, essential programmes and routines must remain. Staff used to working to high standards during term times cannot (and thankfully do not) drop their level of commitment, and overall pressure to do a job well is constant throughout the year.

Organisational features of the extended year at Oaklands

Introductory comments

What follows is a personal viewpoint. It is based on observations and comments from a number of interested parties and is tempered by my own experiences as headteacher at Oaklands since September 1989.

The extended school year throws up many interesting organisational demands and affects every aspect of life at Oaklands. However, the main points noted relate to rotational holiday patterns, supply teacher cover and management issues. Reference is also made to finance and maintenance. It may be that not all these issues are amenable to solution at school level. However, I believe it is ultimately the task of school management to maintain harmony and maximise effectiveness in the best interests of pupils, parents and staff.

Rotational holidays

Teachers work a normal termly pattern: supply teachers replace them during holiday periods: nursery nurses have the same holidays as teachers (54 days) but take them on a rota basis throughout the year. Auxiliaries have 21 days holiday entitlement. There are seven auxiliaries on the staff and fifteen nursery nurses - four of whom are designated 'floaters' and cover for other support staff on holiday. It is at once clear that despite the cited advantage for pupils of educational continuity, the extended year leads to a degree of inbuilt instability in room teams, making consistency of approach difficult.

There is also an increased room management role for class teachers, in organising a constantly changing team and in preparing to hand over to supply teachers. Extra time is needed on communication at all levels. These practical difficulties are exacerbated by the intensity of the educational experience described earlier. Teaching is a closely structured, complicated activity: detailed information exchange is required as staff come and go. This is one reason that the effect of rotational holidays may perhaps be more demanding in a school than in a care establishment.

It is also clear that the extended year further accentuates the difference in conditions of service amongst staff. In most other school settings, auxiliaries would be sessional: although it might be argued that their conditions of service would still be relatively poor, they would at least be on holiday with the rest of the staff. In Oaklands we depend heavily on auxiliaries to support the teaching input as members of specific class teams. Role boundaries tend to become blurred particularly as auxiliaries often find themselves carrying the main thread of continuity in a team simply because they are **there** most of the time. At present, there seem to be no ready solutions in this area.

A further complication of rotational holidays is the increased management time needed in negotiating staff holiday rotas and organising replacements. Staff holidays must be evenly distributed throughout the year since most pupils attend most of the time. We have evolved with the staff a system which encourages 'early booking', allows only four staff off at one time, (as they are covered by four floating staff) and allows only two off in any one class at a time (to maximise class stability). In practice, flexibility and negotiation are the order of the day. It has not been universally easy for staff to accept early booking - after all, it could have been a 'perk' of a sometimes stressful job to be able to take holidays at any time.

In addition, 'floating' is not always a popular role and all room teams have to take their share of change. This will mean keeping staff placements under review and giving 'floaters' the opportunity to be attached to a room team for a period whilst others take on the 'floating' role.

Since our regular teachers hand over to supply teachers for eleven weeks of the year, we have identified a system for passing on information. This is not without snags. The class teacher is required to detail those pupils' programmes that should be carried on during the holiday period and draw up essential information on class routines and individual pupils. Information must be updated regularly. This is a considerable undertaking in addition to other teacher responsibilities. We do not think it appropriate to make fuller records available to supply teachers, simply because they do not have the time, or the background knowledge, to read, digest, and identify for themselves what is essential. This is far better done by the teacher who knows the child well.

This year we have allowed time during 'planned activities' for holiday preparation. However, this limits time for staff development work in a school where enthusiasm for this activity often seems to outstrip energy levels.

The net effect then of rotational holidays can be to fragment the whole staff group making it harder to maintain team spirit as a school. Regular whole school activities help to offset this but a comprehensive communication system is vital. We have developed a network of communication channels in the attempt to ensure a smooth planned flow of information amongst medical staff, education staff and parents. However, there is room for improvement and this system needs constant review and support from school management.

Finally it was the subject of some discussion during the early days of the extended year that teachers might also rotate their holidays. In the event the teachers decided not to alter their conditions of service and now maintain a normal holiday pattern. From my experience so far, I would counsel caution in disrupting this pattern for several reasons:

1.   It would fragment the permanent teaching group.

2.   It would put teachers out of step with regional in-service and risk isolation from colleagues in other schools.

3.   It would make it more difficult to maintain a comprehensive school staff development programme. Well over half of this programme necessarily involves teachers alone. Nursery nurses and auxiliaries join us on in-service days and - by dint of a little judicial hour juggling - on 6 of our 20 planned activity sessions.

4.   It would disrupt the pupil review programme.

5.   It would leave the school with relatively inexperienced supply teachers during term times when educational input is more concentrated.

I believe that class teachers hold a pivotal role in school. They have first line responsibility for co-ordinating pupil information, drawing up educational programmes and managing a room team in the implementing of these programmes. It is therefore vital that they form a cohesive professional team both for their own support and development and to ensure rational curricular and organisational development across the school. In a professional setting, this is never best attempted through top-down decision-making by management. Rotational holidays for the regular teaching force would simply make this more difficult to achieve.

'Holiday' teachers

These come to us through the normal supply channels. Supply teachers tend to have other contractual or family commitments: most are not able to work for long periods during holidays. So far, we have been unable to achieve a really stable teaching force for holidays although, to the Authority's credit, we have never been without cover. Despite the fact that we now have several excellent committed 'regulars' on our holiday list, the holiday supply timetable tends to resemble a patchwork quilt. Some teachers are unprepared for and even unsuited to the work: others will be the first to own that they lack experience and are initially nervous of such a specialist field. A good deal is asked of room staff in supporting teachers particularly when the teacher is regarded as the team leader. It certainly takes an exceptional teacher to offer leadership under these circumstances.

The burden of support is eased slightly by providing supply teachers with a folder of essential information (referred to in the previous section). The folder contains pupil information and guidelines on drugs, safety and practical school routines. Teachers are required to keep a daily diary and an informal register of pupils. The contents of the folder are known to room staff and guidelines have been discussed with them. The folders are issued by the headteacher and discussed with all new supply teachers.

In practice, this discussion is sometimes all too brief as there is reduced management support during school holiday periods and many calls on management time - particularly in the busy early morning period. It is often left largely to the commitment of the teacher in reading and digesting the contents of the folder: she will only have time for this during lunch-time or after school. The commitment will be less if the teacher is only in school for a few days. A more fruitful approach would be through group discussion so that each teacher could properly consider the information and ask questions of the headteacher rather than the beleaguered room staff. This issue needs addressing.

On a more positive note, several teachers who might not otherwise have had the opportunity or motivation to meet pupils with severe and profound needs have developed an interest in the field. This can only benefit the service.

It has also been possible to tighten up on several aspects of school policy and organisation so that support staff know better what to expect and can begin to plan such things as outings in advance of the holiday period.

Finance

Local authority based funding is increased in line with our extended openings and, in common with all other schools, we supplement this by funds raised at school level. Whilst we attempt to maintain essential individual pupil programmes during holiday periods, we also try to develop the leisure side of our provision. Activities include school events and outings. Inevitably then, the holiday periods cost more and since this can be a drain on term-time resources, we rely heavily on fund-raising and donations.

Cleaning and significant maintenance work

These are areas that do not always seize the imagination of educators. However, they are of.crucial importance to the health and well-being of staff and pupils. Where a school is closed only at weekends and on public holidays, problems can arise. This is still being addressed at Oaklands.

Management issues

The extended year increases the role of management: the foregoing text has offered examples of this. Overall, many of the strategies and skills employed by the headteacher become of heightened importance. He/she is responsible for establishing rational planning and evaluation and for coordinating the work of staff and the input of many other agencies against a shifting background. The processes of communication become of vital importance in such a setting and firm leadership must be offered.

It follows that the day to day management of the school cannot and should not be attempted single-handed and needs a team approach. This presents a problem in a small school as the management team is necessarily small.

A complicating issue is that management must take holidays. Since the school must have a representative of the management team on duty at all times, holidays must be staggered. For a school with a headteacher and an assistant head, this means that for twenty six weeks of the year, there will be only one member of 'the team' present. This severely reduces the time available for policy and decision-making.

We have met this to some degree by including the two senior teachers as part of the management team. In this respect we have developed their role in supporting staff development and in offering leadership to others on curricular and room management issues. I feel it is unacceptable and probably unworkable to ask much more of a Senior Teacher. The job remit is largely curriculum based

F

and carries a full class responsibility. However, they do offer support on day to day administrative matters in the temporary absence of the management staff.

During holiday periods this support will not be available. Since the main thrust of management activity is needed during term-time when the regular professional team is present and the educational world is alive, we retain two managers on site as far as possible at this time. There will usually be only one manager available during holiday periods. This often makes it difficult to offer constructive support to supply teachers.

One further effect of staggered management holidays is that it has a tendency to distance the head teacher from his/her normal professional support systems as all meetings with colleagues happen during term-time.

Together these factors pose an interesting scenario for management staff.

Who benefits?

It must be clear from the foregoing that there are many challenging features for a school in offering year round provision. What are the advantages of such a system for pupils and their parents? Are there any disadvantages?

I have not yet tapped the opinions of Oaklands parents extensively. In part, this is because the school is still settling into the extended year. New ways of operating must be negotiated, tried and evaluated. A sense of order and purpose must be established so that any issues can be broached rationally.

Many of our pupils are very demanding both physically and mentally at home. Parents may be more than usually anxious about the well-being, education and long-term future of children with severe and profound special needs because of their dependence and because there seem to be very few specialists that can offer genuine help. 'Care in the community' cannot mean that families shoulder this burden alone or with minimal support. A school like Oaklands might be seen as the 'educational face' of care in the community.

Specifically, Oaklands offers parents more opportunity to attend to other essential aspects of family life by relieving the pressure of care over the long holiday periods. Parents must be easier in their minds if their children are coming to familiar surroundings with familiar staff who know and care for them. They will also be concerned about maintaining their child's educational development: year round school provision must maximise the opportunities for progress.

For some parents, the availability of continued schooling may suggest to them that professional competence outweighs parental competence in the education and care of the child. This is certainly not the case: as with all children, home and school must complement each other: the home environment continues to be a major factor in child development. What about the children? As described, the school is less able to provide continuity than might appear at first sight. Despite this, children are offered a high degree of consistency in their essential learning experiences. They do enjoy coming to school and respond best when important routines are maintained. Holiday periods also offer a range of leisure activities (which, it must be said, the staff appear to enjoy as much as the children!) Therapy and medical services are also available throughout the long holiday periods - although this is perhaps less true of holidays at Christmas and New Year.

I am a little concerned when I note that many of our children are with us most of the year. Despite the need to maintain programmes, all children need a change or a holiday. Children in a special school are often educated well away from their own locality: none of our pupils live in the immediate vicinity of the school. This alone militates against their forming relationships with children who live round about them: it must serve to isolate them further when they come away to school all the time.

What of the future?

The challenge to school and authority in providing year round education has been acknowledged and illustrated. Oaklands is a vibrant place, full of talent, enthusiasm and commitment to the children. It has the capacity to meet the challenge. Despite this, I suspect that year round provision of this nature may put unwarranted pressure on staff and does not work wholly to the advantage of pupils and parents.

I would submit that any future ventures of this sort should include a short closure during the year with full respite and support facilities available to parents through other channels.

The education of children with special needs will increasingly be integrated with that available to their more able peers. If mixed ability schooling is to be on offer to all children, how will this be rationalised with year round educational provision? Will local schools extend their provision? Will respite packages fill the gap? Will special schools continue to offer a backup service? Interesting questions in interesting times!

The Establishment of a Day Centre for Young Adults with Profound Learning Difficulties

Philip Seed

Background

In this chapter I describe how a new centre known as the White Top Centre came to be set up. It can be regarded as a case study of a student-needs led approach to planning in this field, as well as a story of innovation.

Like the majority of innovations for young people with profound and multiple learning difficulties, the initiative came from parents. In this case it was not an organised group of parents, but individuals. In particular, the parents of a multiply disabled young man with cerebral palsy were concerned about what would happen when he left school. This initial concern was matched by the personal interest of Tayside's Regional Director of Social Work, Peter Bates. Tayside already had a new purpose-built Day Centre in Perth (thanks to the generosity of the Gannochy Trust). There was nothing similar in Dundee.

I am not privy to precisely what happened between the parents, the White Top Foundation (which is a local charitable Trust) and Peter Bates. But one day at Aberdeen University, where I was then employed, I received a telephone call from Peter Bates. I was asked to prepare a proposal to undertake at short notice and in eight weeks an exploratory study of the need in Dundee for this group of youngsters. It was stressed that I should have no preconceptions. In due course, I was introduced to the Trustees of the White Top Foundation. Perhaps my own initial contribution and justification for this invitation was that I had previously studied children with very profound learning difficulties at a small special school in Aberdeen (Pitfodels) and at the same time had undertaken a widespread and comprehensive evaluation of day services for adults. (Seed, 1988a)

Exploration

Eight weeks was not a long time to undertake an exploratory study. I spent three weeks becoming familiar with the existing services in Dundee, two weeks reviewing literature and other source materials, one week visiting other places and talking to key people in other parts of Scotland and a final week travelling in England and Wales. I will summarise firstly, the main influences on my thinking as I travelled around, and secondly, the main issues that emerged.

a. Influences

The Scottish Society for the Mentally Handicapped (SSMH) had recently initiated a small specialist provision for adults with profound mental handicaps known as the Carisbrooke Centre at Airdrie. The Centre was started by Karmanie Hastings, since Senior Lecturer in Special Education Department at Lauder Technical College, Dunfermline. When I visited, the manager of the Centre was (and is) Diana Ferguson, who had previously been the Depute. At Carisbrooke I talked to parents and saw for myself that even people with the most profound learning difficulties were capable of learning something new. Some of the young people there seemed to have had better schooling experiences than others. In either case there was a strong argument for a lot of investment, especially of trained and committed staff. For children who have not had good opportunities at school here was a chance to remedy the situation while they were still young. For children who had had good experiences at school here was a chance to continue what had been well started.

Carisbrooke has a lot to teach about methods. The main ingredients are intensive team work, engagement, planning and optimism.

The Carisbrooke Centre is small, catering for just twelve young adults. It occupies an old school building. Another small specialist centre which influenced me in Scotland was the Levern Centre in Priesthill, run by Strathclyde Regional Council Social Work Department, Glasgow South-west District. Here too the SSMH had a hand it setting it up, following a Glasgow-wide survey. Priority was given to those living with elderly single parents and initially there were twelve attenders - subsequently increased to fifteen. Again, it was an adapted building that was available. There was a similar optimism and commitment. I was impressed particularly by the use of informal as well as formal sources of consultancy.

Another centre which had impressed me was the PPAS project in Drumchapel. This was an urban-aided project, again with a very positive outlook and the commitment of parents. It is located in a normal block of Council flats. A particular innovation had been the extension of day time facilities to 24-hour education including the experience of being away from their families. PPAS caters for the full range of adults with learning difficulties but increasingly it was taking adults with more severe learning difficulties.

Other places in Scotland which influenced my thinking positively included Motherwell College of Further Education, whose policy is not to exclude any adult with severe learning difficulties and whose facilities include residential provision. Finally, I was influenced by some of the centres our research team had studied previously, for example, the Victoria Centre, Peebles, where there was a programme of community involvement which included a few people with profound learning difficulties.

G

So what I found was a good base for further innovation in Scotland. Outside Scotland it was a person rather than a place which most influenced me. Judy Sebba, who had long been associated with MENCAP's Profound Retardation and Multiple Handicap project in Manchester and as a Research Fellow in the Hester Adrian Research Centre. She persuaded me to visit the Persondy Centre outside Bridgend in South Wales. Here I met and taped interviews with parents and staff. The story replicated my Scottish experience. Again, this was an adapted school, far from ideal but with plenty of space. A lot of thought had been given to siting, in a neighbourly locality on the outskirts of the town.

I have just mentioned a few of the total number of people and places I contacted - of which there were at least 50. Many of these were in Dundee itself, including for example, Sally Clark, Depute Head of what was then the Fairmuir Unit, now incorporated in Kingspark School, who was a mine of information on educational equipment. Many of my contacts had to be by telephone including telephone trails to get to the root of such issues as whether I should be following the path of conductive education (Sutton, 1989), or Snoezelen equipment (Hulsegge, 1988), or Portage (Cameron, 1986). Then I had to be concerned with specialist aspects and consult, for example in relation to people who are deaf/blind, and be sure that I had the latest information on the relevant treatment issues regarding, for example, epilepsy as well as broader issues such as difficult or so-called 'challenging behaviour' (Blunden, 1989). Of course I did not start 'cold' on many of these issues but there was a lot of updating and probing the boundaries of new knowledge and insights to be undertaken.

In summary I learned from these experiences that learning is possible if there is enough sustained and informed commitment. I am talking about the commitment both of the student and of the staff, although I never cease to be amazed by the commitment to learn on the part of students with profound learning difficulties once they understand that they have an opportunity to learn. Distraction in the training situation has to be coped with constructively but effectively in order to allow maximum engagement and focused learning. 'Room management' techniques provide an effective approach to this problem and the best example of good practice to be found in Scotland is probably at the Carisbrooke Centre. One must work with parents at every stage. A skilled inter-disciplinary staff is all-important. Apart from staff the most important requirement is space. The training provided must be backed by a network of resources. This, in turn, provides resources to others. Other agencies, parents, centres, volunteers and a whole range of experts will all be involved in this network.

b. Issues

If what I have summarised so far provided starting-points, there were a number of issues I had to grapple with. The first related to the definition of the group for whom the facility was intended.

'Profound learning difficulties' is variously interpreted. I am not thinking about an academic discussion of IQs - which are unreliable and not particularly helpful for this group (Seed, 1991). I decided that for our purposes we meant (i) people who were unable to perform most self-management tasks, such as dressing, feeding, toileting or washing without substantial assistance; (ii) most would also have physical impairments and in many cases additional sensory disabilities leading to multiple handicaps; (iii) major communication problems, often without any speech. These were quite stringent criteria but I wanted to narrow it down to those for whom existing provision was manifestly insufficient.

Another issue was whether the proposed provision could be part of an existing day centre or whether it should be entirely separate. The visits I made convinced me that it should be separate. Although there are some good special care units in Scotland, amongst many that are not, attached to adult training centres, for this particular group I can see no argument for artificially putting together people with profound learning difficulties and those with lesser learning difficulties. If we are talking about integration it should surely mean integration between people with learning difficulties, however severe, and ordinary people, places and activities in the community. It is easier to achieve this from a small specialist base than from a larger conglomerate. Experience suggests it is very difficult adequately to target resources on those with the most profound learning difficulties in competition with the needs of students who are more able if both are within the same building and under the same management. Yet for the group we are considering, quality of service is all important. You cannot half train someone to use the toilet or to begin to communicate effectively. A sustained effort based on a high investment of resources is required.

Thirdly, there were issues about the main purposes of the proposed activities. Would these be educational, vocational, recreational or emphasising community involvement - or all of these? My conclusion was that the focus would change but that initially it should be concerned with assessment and training, with appropriate adult involvement in community activities and some recreation. Unlike, for example, the Intogal Project in Ireland (Conneally, 1989) which was a few years ahead of the White Top Centre in its development, it did not seem appropriate to concentrate on training for work, although I appreciate that other projects, especially in England and Wales, have started with this in mind and claim to have achieved success. More ambitious aims could be set once basic training has led to confidence.

Another issue was whether to include hospital patients among those for whom the centre should cater. I was not in favour of this because of the difficulty of transferring learning from a day centre such as we proposed to a hospital ward environment. Eligibility was to be restricted to those living at home or those in small residential units such as those provided in Dundee by Barnardos. I felt that indirectly this would promote pressure to discharge patients more appropriately from hospital knowing that a package of proposed care in the community might include attendance at the centre.

Another issue was the scope of the service. A distinction could be made between a service offering daily provision which I and others felt should be restricted to a small number of attenders, and more widely available consultation to others involved in similar work.

A major question for parents was whether a place at the Centre once granted would be permanent. Parents need a sense of security for their sons or daughters. Yet there are dilemmas here. Firstly, it may prove to be (and I believe it will prove to be) that some of those attending will make more progress than their parents anticipate and that it will be appropriate for them partly or wholly to move on to other generally available services. Secondly - and this was a point that was made strongly by parents of other children still at school and by Sally Clark, for example - if all our resources are put into one small group of people, what about those who are to follow on? This led me later to undertake a small study of the numbers still at school who are likely to be in need of a similar service in the future. For this group the numbers are very small and subject to annual fluctuations. Thus I found at the local school from where most of the children with future requirements will come, the numbers increased as the children got younger. I can foresee pressure for a second centre in a few years' time.

Finally, an important issue was whether the centre should simply be a day centre or whether a residential component should be included. I already mentioned that I was impressed by the PPAS day service in Drumchapel with residential accommodation. This offers students 24-hour training and the experience of being away from home (other than in hospital) for short periods.

The Dundee parents were thinking in terms of appropriate respite, of which there was a lack in the area. I think both sets of needs are important and I therefore proposed that we should talk about a day centre with associated respite. This means that there should be an integrated staff team so that training benefits during the day can be sustained and transferred to overnight situations. This is more sensible than the somewhat artificial 'training flats' for day time use one finds in many adult training centres.

On the question of using ordinary services, going out to a cafe is better than learning table manners in a day centre. This applies to all sorts of other things, from using dental services to hairdressing. But we are talking about people who have to learn very elementary things - or continue to learn these from where they left off at school - relating especially to communication, mobility, motor control, the exercise of choice, sensory perception and interpretation and so on. There has to be an intensive input of human and other resources in an appropriate specialist environment as part of the process of engaging in the ordinary life of the community and interacting with others. Most parents will accept this, some with a degree of scepticism initially perhaps. For them the obvious and immediate benefits are relief, more time for them to spend leading ordinary lives during the day-time at least, relief from isolation and a sense of security for the future.

From concept to proposal

The report of the exploratory study was considered first by the Trustees of the White Top Foundation and then by the Directors or managers of the main statutory departments concerned, including the Health Board, and the Scottish Director of a leading voluntary organisation. After several weeks of deliberation it was agreed that the potential support was sufficient to justify a second stage feasibility study. This was undertaken at a less hurried pace, lasting some six months, with the assistance of David and Irene Anderson, members of the Social Work Department at Dundee University. At this time it also happened that I transferred from Aberdeen to Dundee University Social Work Department. When the feasibility study came to such practical issues as where the building should be sited, the new Head of Dundee University Social Work Department, Professor Bryan Williams suggested a site within the University. The Principal of Dundee University was known to be interested in forging links between the University and the local community and had a particular interest in services for people with disabilities.

The White Top Foundation were keen that the Director of the new centre should be paid a sufficient salary to attract the best person. Since we were now considering a close link with the University I suggested creating a Chair in Multiple Profound Disabilities where the post holder would also be the Director of the Centre. This was accepted by the University Senate on the same day as the proposal for revenue funding was agreed in principle by Tayside Regional Council's Social Work Committee. The latter would provide revenue funding while the White Top Foundation provided the costs associated with the new Director/Chair. So far as I know this is a unique arrangement between a University and a Social Work Department not only in Scotland but in the United Kingdom, although in many ways it parallels long established joint arrangements between Health Boards and Universities. The potential advantages are enormous in bridging the gap between local practice and international expertise.

Two key factors favourably influenced the involvement of the University in the project. The first was the enthusiasm of a wide range of University Departments including Orthopaedic and Traumatic Surgery and its Biomedical Engineering School; Psychiatry; School of Dentistry; Psychology; Medicine; the Micro-computer Centre; and the Department of Social Work itself.It seemed important to pay particular attention to physical aspects of the needs of the young people we were considering. The principle here is that if a person has multiple disabilities, including profound learning difficulties, each of the disabilities should be considered with the same thoroughness as if he or she had fewer or no learning difficulties.

Secondly, the involvement of the University appealed to parents and to the Tayside Regional Social Work Department partly because the University is sited in the centre of the City where there is good access to normal facilities in the community. There might need to be a different form of linkage in the case of a campus university.

Meanwhile, we were working closely with parents to sustain a student-needs led approach. During the exploratory study we had only gained a general idea of the numbers that were likely to be eligible to attend the proposed centre. We now decided to identify who they were and to undertake for planning purposes a preliminary assessment of their needs and potential. Our research team has substantial experience of undertaking feasibility studies to assess needs for local projects. It may be helpful to summarise our approach and methods.

Once the parameters were established - in this case a centre for adults (up to the age of 35) with multiple disabilities, including profound learning difficulties, resident within the City District of Dundee - we asked the relevant key people if they could identify suggested students. Parents had to be approached tactfully. After confirming with agencies or other key people already in contact with potential students, we asked them to arrange an introduction. During this process twenty eight referrals who were potentially suitable were finally reduced to thirteen, who came within the strict terms of reference we had established. It may be noted that while the majority were special school leavers, two of the thirteen had had no substantial services or assessment at all.

We then studied a number of different aspects of each student's home situation including his or her interests and what we called features of performance, the parents' views, social and health history, and hopes for the future. We also asked parents to keep a diary for a fortnight as a basis for studying social networks (Seed, 1990). From all of this information we identified what we called 'growth points' in respect of different aspects of learning potential including physical development. For each growth point we considered implications for staffing, for equipment, for environmental requirements (eg setting and space requirements), implications for transport and for the needs of the main support people at home.

When this had been accomplished for each of the thirteen candidates, the resource implications were summarised providing the basis for considering many different aspects of the centre, especially staffing and the development of the building brief.

Thus the feasibility study was able to specify, not only particular features of the student group - for example that two were totally blind, that a majority suffered from dental problems, a number had epilepsy - but also to indicate the following specific activities envisaged 'for which facilities will need to be available' (though not necessarily all within the centre building):

Basic skills, eg exercise, massage, language and other communication, feeding, toileting and toilet signalling, tactile skills.

Improved positioning - posture.

Sensory awareness and development, eg aromatherapy, garden activities.

Health care, eg dental attention, management of sexual awareness.

Domestic awareness and involvement, eg food preparation.

Community involvement, eg routine visits to shops, sports and places of entertainment.

Social interaction, social awareness and response of familiarisation with different social situations.

At the same time it was appreciated that training methods could not be laid down rigidly in advance. However, this kind of thinking helped us to consider what kind of building we should require and where it should be located.

From proposal to start

The three main areas for further preparation involved working with the parents, finalising the organisational arrangements between the different management and sponsoring organisations involved, and appointing architects. Ideally, the appointment of the Chair would have preceded the appointment of the architects, but the Chair could not be advertised until the organisational arrangements had been finalised and this proved to be quite complicated and time-consuming in such an innovatory setting. There were some very practical management issues that had to be sorted out. We had thought long and hard about the best organisational setting. Professor Chris Cullen, SSMH Professor of Learning Difficulties at St Andrews University, had spoken to me during the exploratory study of what he called "an administrative haven of sanity". The phrase stuck with me as we wrestled with ways to avoid replicating the complex and confusing array of agencies and interests involved during the transition from school to adulthood for people with multiple disabilities and profound learning difficulties. One option might have been to set up a voluntary agency or to invite an existing voluntary agency to run the project. This idea was rejected in favour of the argument for greater financial security from Tayside Regional Council.

The competition for the selection of the architects went ahead in August 1990. I had been responsible for drawing up an architect's brief in collaboration with Wolodmyr Radysh of the Camphill Architects and Bill Pirnie, Senior Lecturer in the Department of Architecture at the Duncan of Jordanstone College of Art. The idea of adapting an existing building, in spite of the advantages which I had suggested in the exploratory study, was rejected in favour of a purpose designed building on a site which is in many ways ideal in a cul-de-sac off the main road just a few minutes' walk away from the main University departments and adjacent to a Hall of Residence and other private housing. A church and a pub are on the corner. It is ten minutes' walk to the centre of the City and open space is also close at hand.

The contract was awarded to a local Dundee firm, who in comparison with their competitors, had relatively little experience in designing buildings for people with disabilities, let alone people with profound and multiple impairments. They won, in my view, on the basis of a touch of brilliance in original design concept and in demonstrating their readiness to undertake detailed research to sustain a student-needs led approach. Thanks to the generosity of the Gannochy Trust as well as the White Top Foundation, £1m was set aside for the cost of the new building.

The design of the building emphasises the interaction between students and the local community. While there are some specialist ideas - for example the hydrotherapy pool - the key note is flexibility and recognition of the need for space. At the same time it has warmth and parts of it even cosiness. It also has made provision for parents, where they wish to be involved and others wishing to visit the Centre. The team of architects has understood and responded to every detail the parents, myself, White Top Trustees, the representative from Tayside Regional Council Social Work Department, the University Buildings Officer and others, including latterly Professor James Hogg, have put to them. They, too, have raised questions on practical issues which we had not necessarily considered. The group met several times and, especially with the inclusion of Professor Hogg, some important changes were made, for example in conceptualising the requirements of staff and where and how these should be met.

Apart from the parents we had worked with from the start, the family support project of Barnardo's in Dundee provided a forum for discussions with a wider group of parents including those whose children were still at school. It was partly their influence which confirmed the need for the centre to be opened during virtually the whole year.

The feasibility study was completed at the end of 1989. It was fifteen months later before the Director, Professor James Hogg, took up his appointment and it is not expected that the building will be operational until late in 1992. An issue here is how to maintain momentum and to keep all the pieces together.

My own role came to an end after a short overlap for handing over information, ideas and the history to Professor Hogg in January 1991. Professor Hogg saw it as one of his very first priorities to get to know each of the families of the prospective students. In this sense the work has begun already. It is important, too, that the core of a staff team at least are able to be appointed and prepared before the centre is fully operational in its unique building.

Professor Hogg will be happy to report on subsequent progress made and welcomes information on, or discussion about, work in progress with people with profound and multiple disabilities. Though providing a service for those individuals identified in Dundee, it is his intention that the White Top Centre should develop wider relations with those involved in this innovative field.

References

Blunden, R and Allen, D (1989). *Facing the Challenge - An Ordinary Life for People with Learning Difficulties and Challenging Behaviour.* Paper No. 74, King's Fund Centre, London.

Cameron, R J (ed). (1986). *Portage - Pre-schoolers, parents and professionals - Ten years of achievement in the UK.* NFER-Nelson.

Conneally, S and Boyle, G (1989). *The Intogel Project - An evaluation of a model of service for adults with a severe and profound mental handicap.* GCAMHC Ltd, The Halls, Quay Street, Galway, Eire.

Hulsegge, J and Verheul, A (1987). *Snoezelen - Another World* (In Britain, further information from Rompa, PO box 5, Wheatbridge Road, Chesterfield, S40 2AE).

Seed, P (1988a). *Children with Profound Handicaps - Parents' Views and Integration.* Falmer Press.

Seed, P (1989b). *Day-care at the Crossroads.* Costello.

Seed, P (1990). *Introducing Network Analysis in Social Work.* Jessica Kingsley.

Seed, P (1991). *Assessment, Resource Allocation and Planning: Literature Review.* University of Dundee Department of Social Work, Publications Service.

Sutton, A (1989). (Telephone conversation). The Foundation for Conductive Education. University of Birmingham (PO Box 363, Birmingham B15 2TT). A centre is also now being developed in Scotland.

Developments in Further Education for Adults with Profound Intellectual and Multiple Disabilities

James Hogg

Introduction

It is significant that people with quite exceptional needs so often find themselves last in the long wait for services and the support they require to lead a life of good quality. The tendency to put them at the margins not only of society in general, but even at the margins of provision for their less needy peers, is an ever present threat that works against this goal. This is nowhere more true than in the case of people whose disabilities embrace not only profound intellectual impairment, but multiple physical and sensory disabilities as well.

If such people have waited long to receive the attention already directed to their more able peers, then there may now be some compensation in the energy and creative thought that is being directed at meeting their needs throughout the course of their lives. While in the United Kingdom generally school-based provision has improved throughout the 1970s and 1980s, it is only in the later years of the 80s that any significant broadly-based thrust to evolve a comprehensive approach to adults with profound and multiple disabilities has come about. In part, this pressure has resulted from the good quality of school service, and the awareness that continuity is essential if the success of the earlier years is to be maintained. For the first time we see emerging a new and comprehensive approach to the curriculum for such adults, a curriculum we would predict will be coherent and widely used in the next five years, subject of course to availability of resources.

For the present writer this emerging situation has special significance, confronting as he does the opportunity to establish a new day-service for such adults in Dundee, the White Top Centre. Seed, in Chapter 12, has described the research undertaken as a prerequisite to establishing this Centre. Though the Centre will not be open until early in 1993, attention is being devoted at present to the form that the service will take, and particularly to the way in which the curriculum is conceived and organised. In approaching this subject, I have been acutely aware of the important strides already made in Scotland and elsewhere. Here in Scotland there are now a number of services for adults with profound intellectual and multiple disabilities that have proved highly innovative, including the Carisbrook Centre (Hastings 1988), the Kinnoull Centre, Perth, Motherwell Further Education College and the Levern Centre, Glasgow. All had some input during Seed's research into the development of the White Top Centre. In England and Wales, the Further Education Unit, a national body related to the Department of Education & Science, is also involved in a full review of the issue of further education for this group. (FEU 1991)

This paper is a preliminary attempt to draw together some of the main elements that I believe should go to make up a comprehensive service for people with profound intellectual and multiple disabilities as reflected in these wider initiatives. Implicitly, it might be viewed as a preliminary statement on the direction which the White Top Centre will initially take, to be evolved through the experience and aims of future colleagues yet to be appointed, and more detailed discussions with parents and carers of prospective service users.

The paper is organised around four themes, themselves inextricably linked. These are:

> First, about whom are we talking? and, how do we view the person with multiple disabilities, with particular reference to the relation between choice and quality of life?

> Second, how should a further education curriculum for adults with profound difficulties be formulated?

> Third, what is the form and content of such a curriculum?

> Fourth, how do we administer curriculum implementation?

1. About whom are we talking?

There can never have been a time when those of us working in the UK in the field of disability have got ourselves into such confusion over the issue of terminology, to the point now where discussion with North American or European colleagues is at times nigh on impossible. That these attempts to redefine terminology are well-intentioned cannot be denied; the extent to which they have been carefully reflected on is less apparent. With respect to the group of concern in this paper, it is interesting to take a selection of terms applied to them in just a handful of articles that have recently appeared (Figure 1).

Figure 1. Examples of terminology applied in recent publications.
People with:

Profound and Multiple Disabilities
Profound Disabilities
Profound Cognitive Impairment
Profound and Multiple Learning Difficulties (PMLD)
Profound Intellectual Disability
Profound and Complex Difficulties
Profound and Complex Learning Difficulties
Profound Retardation and Multiple Handicaps
Profound and Multiple Impairments
Profound Intellectual Disability and Additional Physical and/or Sensory
Disabilities
Special Needs Clients
Profound/Complex Physical and Learning Difficulties

It would be wearisome to go through Figure 1 and discuss the acceptability of each term. Perhaps the only one which does merit comment is the widely accepted 'Profound and Multiple Learning Difficulties' (PMLD), (at least in the school population). For the purposes of this paper, this term was rejected on three grounds. First, the term 'learning difficulties' is a misnomer. We are talking here of people with extensive intellectual problems that embrace, yes, learning, but also perception, information processing, memory, motivation and so on. This extensiveness is not covered by the apparently innocuous term 'learning', which in this context can most kindly be described as euphemistic. Second, the term 'difficulties' seems a travesty of English usage when applied to individuals whose intellectual problems stem from often massive brain damage or abnormality, with consequent serious medical and physical sequelae. Third, the term 'learning difficulties' seems particularly demeaning to adults when it is borne in mind that it is a term extrapolated from a report on school children (Department of Education and Science, 1978). It would be a little like referring to a college student as a 'pupil'. Fourth, the term 'PMLD' to imply that the multiple 'difficulties' are essentially 'learning' in nature is incorrect. While, of course, having spastic quadriplegia and absence of vision have profound consequences for learning, it is inaccurate to subsume them under the term 'multiple learning difficulties'.

Our chosen terminology can readily be seen to be the corollary of these objections to 'PMLD'. First, instead of the inappropriate term 'learning' we have opted for 'intellectual', qualifying the extent of intellectual disability with 'profound' as in PMLD. By 'intellectual' we are referring to the outcome of a variety of psychological and experiential processes that enable a person to understand and act appropriately in relation to the world in which they live. We have chosen 'disability' as a widely used and accepted term in international classification systems, e.g. World Health Organisation (1980), where a disability is the consequence of an impairment to physical or mental performance imposing constraints on the individual's functioning, though not necessarily with handicapping consequences.

We have separated intellectual from 'multiple disabilities' where 'multiple' refers to physical and/or sensory disabilities. In full we would choose to use 'profound intellectual disability and multiple physical and/or sensory disabilities', though less cumbersomely we will use the shorthand 'profound intellectual and multiple disabilities', as we have in our title and the opening paragraphs of this chapter.

We will also refer to 'people with profound intellectual and multiple disabilities', though in particular cases 'service users', 'clients' or 'consumers' might be used, or even 'students' or 'trainees', depending on the context.

How do we view the person with profound intellectual and multiple disabilities?

Within current policy in the field of disability, i.e. with respect to both educational provision and community care initiatives, people with profound intellectual and multiple disabilities have the same legislated rights and entitlements as their more able peers. In broad terms society should enable them to lead a normalised life in the community (Wolfensberger 1972), informed by the philosophy of social role valorisation. In reality, however, we are all aware of entrenched views even among those providing educational or social services which are quite contrary to such a philosophical position. In recent months I have heard a professional advocate automatic sterilisation of all girls with profound and multiple disabilities at the age of twelve years, and another urge that too great an effort is put into maintaining the lives of such people who ".....in any way won't see their teens out." I have witnessed the total unwillingness (not inability) of some members of an organisation devoted to leisure provision for those with multiple disabilities. I have seen a major training establishment demand the withdrawal of a twenty year old young woman with multiple disabilities from their establishment within two weeks of her arrival, though lip-service to making provision in that establishment for such people has never wavered in public. In the last week I have been told of young people with profound disabilities being removed from their hostel with the furniture being taken out from around them before they left, and being transported to unknown destinations while having major seizures. To be told by care staff that a chair specifically designed to minimise the development of scoliosis is not being used because of a distaste for its appearance is as much irresponsible in its failure to serve the person with disabilities, as it is a misunderstanding of what 'normalisation' entails.

We have, then, the philosophy; if it is to be more than self-justifying rhetoric the values must be translated at every step into practical realisation of these beliefs to which we all pay lip service. As a practical starting point for viewing the way in which we enhance the lives of people with profound intellectual and multiple disabilities, I would like to take the concept of quality of life as my starting point. This is a concept that is receiving increasing attention in the attempt to evaluate services and undertake research into the impact of the world on people with disabilities. Brown, Bayer and MacFarlane (1989) comment that quality of life is determined by an interaction between the individual and the environment. They go on: 'It can be described in terms of personal control that can be exerted by the individual over the environment. It must be assessed by consulting the individual directly ....The larger the gap between attainment and needs or wants, the poorer generally is the quality of life'. Then we must ask ourselves how we are to assess quality of life in the lives of people with profound and multiple disabilities.

In the extensive literature on the assessment of quality of life, two distinguishable, but in reality related, aspects need to be considered. The first of these, which was studied over half a century ago by Thorndike (1939), used observable indicators that can be assessed without direct reference to the person being considered. Such measures may include services received, access to community activities and so on. Program Analysis of Service Systems (PASS), (Wolfensberger & Thomas 1983), though formulated to assess the degree to which normalisation criteria are being met, is one such 'objective' instrument. The authors are quite explicit in laying no claim to the effects of the normalised environment on a person's perception of its value to them. It has long been realised, however, that there is a psychological dimension to quality of life which requires that we 'gain an understanding of the life quality felt, processed, and acted upon by each individual' (Zautra 1983). With respect to service provision in general for people with profound and multiple disabilities, and with regard to the setting of curriculum objectives in particular, therefore, reference to the outcome of successful intervention in relation to life quality is a crucial consideration.

What are the essential components that contribute to this global idea of life quality? The first, multi-faceted contribution, is systematic assessment followed by intervention informed by the outcome of the assessments. Specifically, comprehensive psychological, social, physical, sensory, medical and environmental assessment constitute the basis on which all intervention ultimately proceeds. While this may seem to be a statement of the obvious, it is quite apparent that appropriate assessment is not the norm in many educational and intervention settings for people with profound and multiple disabilities. Even in the area of sensory assessment, Hogg & Lambe's (1988) survey found nine per cent of children's parents and carers and eight per cent of those of adults had not received assessment information as to whether their son or daughter had visual impairment. The equivalent figure for hearing impairment for both groups was four per cent. Clinical experience would suggest that all these figures are considerable underestimates. Similarly, one observes, year by year, the physical mismanagement of individuals who become visibly deformed as a result of failure to assess their physical needs. It is still not unusual to visit schools in which no developmental or psychological assessment has ever been undertaken, and in which teachers confuse the important activity of their 'getting to know' a person with the activity of such assessment. Where assessment has been considered, all too often *ad hoc* instruments have been developed by well-intentioned staff. We have argued elsewhere (Hogg & Raynes 1987) that all staff involved in intervention should be critically appraising the multiplicity of assessment instruments now available, rather than re-inventing the wheel in the form of such unstandardised instruments devised for their own facilities.

If we consider social and environmental assessment then measures of community involvement and environmental suitability and quality will be entailed. In the former careful measures were taken on the extent to which adults, including those with profound disabilities, not only lived in the community, but actually participated in the various activities available. PASS evaluation draws our attention to a range of aspects of the kind of environment provided that may enhance a person's image as a valued person.

The second component of such 'extrinsic' assessment is that the assessment has not only been undertaken but acted on. Beyond the required aids and adaptations to the person's environment that physical-medical assessment might require, we are led to consider the teaching and experiential interventions that will be required. Here, outcomes relate to changes in understanding and acting that lead to independence and greater control of the environment. It is this issue that we take up later in our discussion of curriculum development.

Against this background of *extrinsic* determinants of quality of life, we must also assess and act upon *intrinsic* aspects leading us to examine three related concepts, i.e *affective experience*, with its implications for *choice* and *self-determination*.

Affective experience

By 'affective experience' we are referring to the emotional state of the person with profound and multiple disabilities. It is apparent that education in western civilisation has in the main emphasised intellectual experience and the acquisition of knowledge at the expense of the emotional development of pupils and students. Where affective experience has been acknowledged, it has been secondary to the main purpose of education which is to impart knowledge and skills.

In our earlier books (Hogg & Sebba 1986a;b) we make virtually no explicit reference to emotional development, or to the idea that assessment of the emotional state of a person with profound and multiple disabilities is as central as assessing 'fine motor' or 'cognitive' development. In many respects this omission reflected the state of this field at the time we were writing. Though developmental psychology has in recent years emphasised the importance of affective development (e.g. Trevarthen 1984), it is only recently that affect has become a central concern in the field of profound and multiple disability. Two primary reasons may be suggested. First, there has been a growing interest in communication in people with profound and multiple disability, which is developmentally frequently 'pre-verbal'. Pre-verbal communication may be viewed not only in terms of its pragmatic function, i.e. the intended outcome of a communication such as inducing an adult to retrieve a toy, but with respect to its emotional expression of the individual's state. Second, an interest in the emotional state for its own sake in people with profound disabilities has recently emerged. Since it is the well-being, as well as the abilities, of the person with which we should be concerning ourselves, how can we sensitively detect changes in the mood or emotional state of the person?

It is beyond the scope of this chapter to offer a detailed account of affect in people with profound and multiple disabilities further. Latchford (1989), in a recent thesis undertaken at Edinburgh University, and Withers (1991), have demonstrated the feasibility of observing and recording emotional expression in people with profound disabilities, the latter showing how ratings of affect can reliably distinguish the reaction people with profound disabilities make to different situations. Extensive work, too, is now being undertaken in the USA into behavioural states in people with profound disabilities, of which Guess *et al.* (1991) provide an important recent example.

Choice
Recent Community Care legislation has placed an increasing emphasis on preference and choice of those using services. For many people with profound disabilities any conventional expression of choice will not be feasible. However, this situation does not mean that the concept of choice is any less relevant. It must, however, be explored through careful observation of activities and experiences selected when opportunities for choice are presented. Preference may be demonstrated motorically, e.g. through a preferred object being reached for, or through attention, eg a preferred source of stimulation being attended to for a longer period than a less preferred object. It will readily be seen as well that choice as expressed through positive affect or behavioural state is also feasible employing observational techniques of the sort described in the previous paragraph.

Self-determination
If we are to attend to choice in adults with profound disabilities and enable them

to determine the quality of their lives by responding to expressed preferences, we must consider the implications when that choice is contrary to what an extrinsic assessment may have determined. A preference for inactivity that may lead to increased deformity may run counter to what our assessments tell us is 'in the best interest' of the person. There is no simple answer to what is a genuine paradox, i.e. that sometimes what a person wants and what is best for her or him are incompatible. It has been suggested that one approach to the problem is that developing the ability to make choices should become part of the overall curriculum with people being taught to make choices (Bannerman, Sheldon, Sherman & Harchik 1990) as a central activity.

This final point returns us to the dual nature of assessing quality of life, i.e. through assessment of the service received and the expressed views and feelings of the person using the service. We would argue that in services for people with profound and multiple disabilities, both components should be inherent parts of evaluating our service, a major task that will be undertaken by White Top Centre staff in the development of that service.

2. How should a further education curriculum for adults with profound disabilities be formulated?

Historically, day services and further educational provision have only recently been extended to adults with profound and multiple disabilities. In many parts of the UK such services remain non-existent or offer only an inadequate and under-resourced service. The attempt to improve the quality of such services through the development of carefully conceived curricula is even more recent. This development, a natural extension of the school experience of most young people with profound disabilities, has received a considerable impetus through the development of further education initiatives for people with profound and multiple disabilities. In the Department of Education & Science's (DES) Further Education Unit's document, 'Adult Status for All? Continuing education for people with profound and multiple disabilities' (FEU 1991) the issues underlying such a curriculum are addressed. It is noted that:

> Continuing education should aim to meet these needs by offering an individually tailored education programme within a properly constructed curriculum framework, which uses age-appropriate activities, language, materials and teaching strategies. Technological support has a vital part to play. Such a programme will stretch and challenge the learner within a supportive setting.

In recent years the content and form of the curriculum for both children and adults with profound and multiple disabilities has received growing attention (e.g.

Orchard Hill Further Education Centre (ND), Hertfordshire County Council Curriculum (ND)). With respect to core content there is considerable agreement among several sources which have suggested content. While a finer division could be made, seven key areas may be suggested:

Cognition: i.e. the development of an understanding of the relations between objects, their place in space, causality in relation to objects and people.

Communication: with particular reference to the use of verbal and non-verbal communication to influence the world, as well as the expression of emotion as a communicative act.

Social behaviour: particularly with respect to awareness of others and sequencing of social acts.

Adaptive behaviour: typically with reference to diverse self-help activities ranging through self-feeding and drinking, coping with hygiene needs, self-dressing etc.

Movement: both with respect to 'fine' (hand and finger) and 'gross' (bodily posture and movement) motor activities.

Choice: as noted above, to be seen as part of the curriculum as well as a determinant of the person's life. Choice needs to be taught and refined in order to optimise decision-making.

Affective development: i.e. increasing emotional growth and experience.

To these areas should be added the natural extension of affective experience, namely sensory and aesthetic experience. In these areas particularly recent years have seen a marked expansion with the development of multisensory environments (e.g. sensory gardens, Lambe 1991a; Snoezelen, Hulsegge & Verheul 1987; Galaxies, published by the Consortium, ILEA 1984) as well as the use of reflexology, aromatherapy etc (topics covered comprehensively in Lambe 1991b). These divisions, however, should be maintained only in order to assist us in keeping clearly in mind the **diversity** of aims with which we should be concerned. It is important to emphasise that with respect to the activity of teaching, they are in reality inseparable. We would wish to argue for a whole-person approach to education with people with profound disabilities, an approach which has significant practical implications for how we devise teaching situations, what happens within them, and how we record and evaluate our activities, a philosophy to which we return below.

The criterion for the teaching of any activity should be the usefulness of the newly acquired behaviour in the wider environment, referred to as 'the criterion of ultimate function'. Such outcomes are conceived in the FEU (1991) document in relation to increased independence, enhanced dignity and improved opportunities to be with other adults.

Though concerned with school age pupils, the development of the National Curriculum in relation to children with severe and profound learning difficulties should provide an important stimulus in relation to further education practice. Ouvry (1991) offers a detailed consideration of the National Curriculum in relation to pupils with profound disabilities, also emphasising holistic approaches to teaching. The National Curriculum Council (1991a) provide full curriculum guidance on the National Curriculum and severe intellectual disabilities. In addition, a variety of detailed documents are at present emerging which are also relevant to older students with profound disabilities. In 'Entitlement for All in Practice: A broad, balanced and relevant curriculum for pupils with severe and complex learning difficulties in the 1990s' (Fagg, Aherne, Skelton and Thorber 1990) the authors set the scene for the development of a National Curriculum from which pupils with intellectual disabilities will not be excluded. In parallel documents on the science, mathematics and communication curricula provide clear statements of the content and aims of these areas. (Fagg, Skelton, Aherne & Thorber 1990; Aherne, Thorber, Fagg & Skelton 1990a; Aherne, Thorber, Fagg & Skelton 1990b). Ackerman & Mount (1991) and Mount & Ackerman (1991) deal respectively with literacy and technology. Within this reappraisal of the curriculum, an emphasis on integration across subject areas is very apparent, and quite consistent with the holistic approach advocated above. Thus, Byers (1990) eloquently describes the use of teaching by topic with an example of the use of developing a garden as a focus for a wide range of curriculum activities for pupils of differing abilities. National Curriculum Council (1991b) show how the topic of 'Water' can act as a focus for an integrated scheme of work.

3. What is the form and content of such a curriculum?

Two sources may be identified for most assessment and curriculum instruments that have been developed during the 1970s and 1980s: first, with little argument, the primary **documented** source of much development in the field of profound disability has been applied behaviour analysis, and has entailed the introduction of behavioural methods into this field. Central to such an approach has been the careful specification of behavioural objectives in some of the over-arching curriculum areas noted above (specifically, cognition, communication, social and adaptive behaviour, with choice being subsumed under 'reinforcer/reward preference' and affective behaviour generally being contained within pre-verbal communication checklists). Each area has been divided into sequences of behaviours with earlier items being assumed logically and/or functionally to precede later items. Such behavioural checklists have sometimes been presented in a more complex fashion as in the matrices of Bricker & Bricker (1974) or Kiernan & Jones (1982), or subjected to complex task analyses deriving from industrial task analysis procedures (Hogg 1981). The second source derives from the innovatory work in the UK of Woodward viewing the behaviour of children with profound disabilities from a Piagetian perspective (e.g. Woodward 1959, and reviewed by Hogg & Sebba 1986a, Woodward 1979). This highly original and sadly undervalued series of studies may subsequently have been eclipsed by publication of the Uzgiris-Hunt Ordinal Scales of Infant Development (Uzgiris & Hunt 1975) and the even more formalised version produced by Dunst (1980). These scales have facilitated the wider application of Piagetian theory to provide a theoretical framework for curriculum content. While conceptually some behavioural psychologists would argue against any *rapprochement* between behavioural and Piagetian theory, in reality there are several well documented studies suggesting that the two approaches can be brought into a mutually beneficial relation. (For a discussion of this issue see Hogg & Sebba 1986a.)

Elsewhere we have reviewed the checklist and matrix-based procedures to assessment (Hogg & Sebba 1986b) and considered the relation between such assessment and curricula that were at the time available (Hogg & Sebba 1986b), summarising in tabular form some thirteen curricula relevant to people with profound and multiple disabilities. Several of these are explicitly informed by Piagetian theory, and in some cases have assimilated research on language and communicative development. In considering after an interval of some five years these curricula and their underlying assessment checklists in relation to the development of an adult curriculum, two central criticisms are apparent. First, in the justifiable attempt to set identifiable teaching objectives they have typically led to a highly fragmented approach to the individuals with whom we are concerned, quite inconsistent with the whole-person approach advocated above. Second, as Bray, MacArthur & Ballard (1988) note, such objectives are set, and movement towards meeting them controlled, by teachers and instructors. These authors emphasise a more interactive approach in which teacher/instructor behaviour is itself directed by the student/learner. Though they have not yet been widely disseminated, such interactive approaches have received increasing attention over the past few years. Thus, working in Scotland, Burford (1988) has investigated rhythmic actions for engagement in people with profound disabilities, making a demonstration tape widely available. In the USA, Gleason (1988) has emphasised the need to analyse and act sensitively towards social interactions of some complexity, especially where they involve people with profound disabilities.

These criticisms do not in any sense argue for the abandonment of a careful specification of objectives or of behavioural methods, a point acknowledged by

Bray *et al.* (1988). However, reformulation of both assessment and educational approach are called for, with consequences for recording and the way in which the various professions work together. This critique of 'checklist-style' curricula can be made less abstract by a consideration of a more recent curriculum for children and adults with profound and multiple disabilities. 'The Kidderminster Curriculum: for children and adults with profound and multiple learning difficulties' (Jones 1989a) is a meticulously prepared and presented handbook accompanied by an easily used Kidderminster Curriculum Assessment Checklist. This curriculum goes well beyond existing approaches in giving consideration to teacher targets as well as student targets, and, as we shall show, begins to take steps towards proposing a more integrated approach to the person with profound disabilities. It remains, however, a traditional, checklist-orientated approach to the curriculum, solidly akin to those reviewed by Hogg & Sebba (1986b). Core areas covered are self-help, gross motor, fine motor, socialisation and communication and play, with the last area weakest and perhaps unnecessarily conflating aspects of cognition, sensory functioning, play, and leisure (the last covered by only four items).

What is of particular interest to our present argument, however, is that recommendations are taken towards integrating separate core areas within individual teaching programmes. Thus the need to consider gross motor behaviour (specifically posture and head control) when dealing with self-help objectives such as eating is emphasised. Similarly, when considering gross motor behaviour, such as basic body control, attention is drawn to functional possibilities:

> Although many of the targets in this component are isolated
> movements rather than functional skills, they can be made functional
> by capitalising on whatever movements are possible via the use of
> specialised switches and aids. (Jones, 1989a)

Several other examples may be given ranging from the adaptive function of mouth co-ordination to the relation of communication and choice. Similarly the involvement of professions such as physiotherapy are suggested, with reference to teacher targets (i.e. the teacher should collect certain specific information from a physiotherapist) and with respect to the part played by advice from physiotherapists in programme development.

The value of this curriculum to staff, particularly those with limited training, cannot be doubted. However, it is equally clear that future developments must lead to curricula that specify far more explicitly the procedures required to integrate core areas in activities with individual students. It is not difficult to envisage an analysis of a specific situation in which several core areas are brought together. Thus, taking Jones' example, a feeding programme cannot be formulated independently of considerations of posture and positioning, but nor can the sensory and cognitive aspects of the situation be ignored. Vision, hearing, touch, and understanding of the relation between objects are all implicit in the situation, as is communication between people at meal time, and the affective aspects of those interactions and the enjoyment of food and drink. Viewed in this way, the learning situation might embrace checklist items from all core areas, and would demand input from all professionals concerned in the service. Bray *et al.* (1989) emphasise, however, that appropriate learning situations should also emerge from the social and other needs expressed by the student. Enjoyment of a particular activity, e.g. visiting the beach, can equally be conceived as an opportunity to introduce in an integrated context these various curriculum elements. The one constraint that must always figure, is that the activity and its outcome demonstrably enhance the individual's quality of life which should also be defined as part of the wider programme aims.

The strength of such an approach, and indeed, some of the complex issues it raises are well illustrated in the application at Gogarburn School of Nind & Hewett's (1988) approach to interactive teaching reported on by Knight & Watson (1990). As with cognitively orientated aspects of the curriculum described above, interactive teaching's theoretical starting point is in child development theory. Here, however, it is the study of early mother-child interaction and the development of communication from which the approach derives. As Knight & Watson observe:

> In this curriculum model we are trying to analyse skills used in infant-parent interaction and apply them to our situations. It does **not** mean treating our pupils like babies. It is very important to respect their chronological age and to recognise that their life experience is very different from that of babies. However in order to give them the best possible opportunity to develop, and to facilitate the best level of communication they are capable of, we have to use all methods at our disposal, and this is one which seems to work. We call it **intensive interaction** and it consists of a member of staff working one-to-one with a pupil, concentrating all their attention on that pupil, and initially observing, and responding to any movement, expression or sound given by the pupil. The member of staff is not **teaching** in a traditional sense, but responding creatively to the pupil. In doing so she will often use the techniques described which are part of parent-child interaction. Gradually games and sequences will emerge which the staff member will use and expand. The purpose of the games is to build a communicative relationship, and in so doing promote such things as pupil initiations, eye-contact, turn-taking, understanding cause and effect. Underlying all activities is the recognition of the

importance of the pupil being an active partner in the engagement, consciously trying to move from the pupil as passive, and staff member as active paradigm. (Knight & Watson, 1990)

The term 'intensive interaction' might be deemed an inappropriate one. Intensity *per se* has little to do with the quality of interactions. Indeed, one cannot imagine a more intensive interaction than that which takes place between a behaviour modifier engaged in over-correction and the reluctant recipient of over-correction. A more appropriate designation might be 'responsive interaction' where the emphasis is on response to the student. Underlying this approach is the belief that in such an interactive setting, 'emergent goals' will be identified that for several reasons are deemed more valid than objectives set in more behaviourally orientated (though not necessarily theoretically behavioural) approaches. Thus, emergent goals imply child-centredness rather than goal-centredness, a predominantly non-linguistic teaching context, utilising intrinsic motivation and the increased probability of wide generalisation because the interactions are free of any particular setting.

While Knight & Watson provide a valuable description of the use of the approach which is highly consistent with holistic, client-centred methods, several crucial issues have yet to be addressed. First, how do we identify a given aspect of the person's self-initiated behaviour as constituting an appropriate educational objective? This is important because (a) not all such behaviour is going to provide an emergent goal, and (b) without answering this question it is impossible to establish any direction to the teaching or know when a goal has been achieved. Second, how far removed from more traditional approaches is interactive teaching? It is interesting to note that several of the behaviours that constitute emergent goals are just those referred to in other more formal curricula, e.g. 'understanding of cause and effect'. In other words, teachers have an implicit cognitive curriculum based on the same developmental models as underpin those reviewed by Hogg & Sebba. What appears to be different is the sensitivity to behaviour exhibited by the child in an interactive situation, as distinct from formal testing or direct observation. The emergence of interactive teaching does not render any less pressing the overall issues that still need to be addressed in the wider field of education for adults, to which we now turn.

To develop the curriculum for people with profound and multiple disabilities in the holistic way that is being urged on all sides requires several developmental stages:

(i) assessment instruments that embody the inter-relations between core areas and specific objectives will have to be devised. Such instruments if developed as criterion-referenced assessments will also provide a vehicle for recording and curriculum evaluation

(ii)   assessment will need to embrace the elements of choice and personal expression through affective and behavioural states. The important implication of this requirement is that much assessment will not fit comfortably into a pre-designed package (e.g. Portage, Kidderminster Curriculum etc) but will require creative interpretation and re-interpretation by those working with the student

(iii)   implementation will require genuine interdisciplinary activity, with respect to assessments being undertaken jointly by educational, therapeutic and habilitation staff in a common context, and teaching carried out collaboratively by teaching, and integrated record keeping. The presence of a variety of professionals in the same service setting in no way guarantees such interdisciplinary collaboration. In order to avoid purely rhetorical claims that such collaboration is occurring, this activity needs to be documented and embodied in the whole curriculum implementation process

Conclusion

The development of an integrated curriculum of the kind described will have important implications at the organisational and operational levels. Such an approach cannot be divorced from such considerations. While respecting and preserving the expertise of individual educators, therapists and other staff, the curriculum's implementation will entail considerable flexibility on the part of staff and an openness to evolving their own practices in sometimes novel ways. No room is left for the kind of professionalism which prefers to operate in isolation, or assumes that a particular profession can take over new areas of activity without reference to existing expertise in a given area.

Given the breadth of the potential curriculum and the need to locate activities in a wider community setting, care will need to be taken to ensure that the critical non-Centre environment in which people live, i.e. their home, and a variety of community settings, is embraced within the total approach. The involvement of parents, while differing from family to family, should therefore be integral to planning. The differing legal status of guardianship for adults in Scotland from that pertaining in England and Wales effectively requires that this relationship with the family is central. It is also a distinct advantage in that the relationship is clearly formulated and many of the difficulties now existing in adult services in relation to service provision for adults in England and Wales can be avoided.

References

Ackerman, D and Mount, M (1991). *Literacy for All.* David Fulton.

Aherne, P, Thorber, A, Fagg, S and Skelton, S (1990a). *Mathematics for All: an interactive approach to level 1.* David Fulton.

Aherne, P, Thorber, A, Fagg, S and Skelton, S (1990b). *Communication for All: a cross-curricular skill involving interactions between 'Speaker and Listener'.* David Fulton.

Bannerman, D, Sheldon, J B, Sherman, J A and Harchik, A E (1990). Balancing the right to habilitation with the right to personal liberties: The rights of people with developmental disabilities to eat too many doughnuts and take a nap. *Journal of Applied Behaviour Analysis,* 23.

Bray, A, MacArthur, J and Ballard, K D (1988). Education for pupils with profound disabilities: Issues of policy, curriculum, teaching methods, and evaluation, *European Journal of Special Educational Needs,* 3.

Bricker, W A & Bricker, D D (1974). An early language training strategy, in R L Schiefelbusch and L L Lloyd (eds). *Language Perspectives: Acquisition, retardation and intervention.* University Park Press.

Brown, R I, Bayer, M B & MacFarlane, C (1989). Rehabilitation *Programmes: Performance and quality of life of adults with developmental handicaps.* Lugus.

Burford, B (1988). Action cycles: Rhythmic actions for engagement with children and young adults with profound mental handicap, *European Journal of Special Educational Needs,* 3.

Byers, R (1990). Topics: From myths to objectives, *British Journal of Special Education,* 17.

Consortium, ILEA (1984). *Galaxies.* ILEA.

Dunst, C J (1980). *A Clinical and Educational Manual for Use with Uzgiris and Hunt Scales of Infant Psychological Development.* Pro-Ed.

Fagg, S, Aherne, P, Skelton, S and Thorber, A (1990). *Entitlement for All in Practice: A broad, balanced and relevant curriculum for pupils with severe and complex learning difficulties in the 1990s.* David Fulton.

Fagg, S, Skelton, S, Aherne, P and Thorber, A (1990). *Science for All*. David Fulton.

Further Education Unit (1991). *Adult Status for All? Continuing education for people with profound and multiple disabilities. A discussion paper*, FEU.

Gleason, J (1988). Intent on play: Social-cultural dimension of the group life of person with profound developmental disabilities. *European Journal of Special Educational Needs*, 3.

Guess, D, Roberts, S, Siegel-Causey, E, Ault, M, Guy, B, Thompson, B, Rues, J, Siegel-Causey, D and Wooster, B (1991). *Investigations into the State Behaviour of Students with Severe and Profound Handicapping Conditions*. University of Kansas.

Hastings, K (1988). Carisbrooke people can: A positive structured approach to the development of adults with profound and multiple impairments. *European Journal of Special Educational Needs*, 3.

Hertfordshire County Council (ND). *A Framework for Learning for People with Profound and Complex Learning Difficulties*.

Hogg, J (1981). Learning, using and generalising manipulative skills in a preschool classroom by nonhandicapped and Down's syndrome children. *Educational Psychology*, 1.

Hogg, J and Lambe, L J (1988). *Sons and Daughters with Profound Retardation and Multiple Handicaps Attending Schools and Social Education Centres: Final Report*. Royal Society of Mentally Handicapped Children and Adults, London.

Hogg, J and Raynes, N V (1987). Assessing people with mental handicap: An introduction, in J. Hogg and N.V. Raynes (eds) *Assessment in mental handicap: A guide to assessment practices, tests and checklists*. Croom Helm.

Hogg, J and Sebba, J (1986a). *Profound Retardation and Multiple Impairment: Volume 1: Development & training*. Chapman & Hall.

Hulsegge, J and Verheul, A (1987). *Snoezelen: Another world*. Rompa.

Jones, L (1989a). *The Kidderminster Curriculum: for Children and adults with profound and multiple learning difficulties*. School of Psychology, University of Birmingham.

Jones, L (1989b). *Assessment Checklist for The Kidderminster Curriculum: for Children and adults with profound and multiple learning difficulties.* School of Psychology, University of Birmingham.

Kiernan, C C and Jones, M (1982). *The Behaviour Assessment Battery,* NFER- Nelson.

Knight, C and Watson, J (1990). *Intensive Interactive Teaching at Gogarburn School.* Moray House College, Edinburgh.

Lambe, L (1991a). *A Leisure Resource Training Pack for Use with people with Profound Intellectual and Multiple Disabilities.* MENCAP.

Lambe, L (1991b). Developing a sensory garden. In L. Lambe (ed) *A Leisure Resource Training Pack for Use with people with Profound Intellectual and Multiple Disabilities.* MENCAP.

Latchford, G (1989). *Towards an Understanding of Profound Mental Handicap.* Unpublished PhD Thesis, University of Edinburgh.

Mount, M and Ackerman, D (1991). *Technology for All.* David Fulton.

National Curriculum Council (1991a). *National Curriculum and Pupils with Severe Learning Difficulties.* NCC.

Nind, M and Hewett, D (1988). Interaction as curriculum, *British Journal of Special Education,* 15.

Orchard Hill Further Education Centre (ND). *Orchard Hill Further Education Centre: Prospectus.* St Mary's Hospital, London.

Ouvry, C. (1991). Access for pupils with profound and multiple learning difficulties, in R. Ashdown, B. Carpenter and K. Bovair (eds), *The Curriculum Challenge: Access to the National Curriculum for pupils with learning difficulties.* Falmer.

Sebba, J, Galloway, S, and Rodbard, G (1991). *'Water': An integrated approach to meeting the needs of pupils with profound and multiple learning difficulties within the National Curriculum.* Hertfordshire County Council.

Trevarthen, C (1984). Emotions in infancy: Regulators of contact and relationships with persons, in K. R. Sherer & P. Ekman (eds) *Approaches to Emotion.* Lawrence Erlbaum.

Thorndike, E. L (1939). *Your City.* Harcourt, Brace & Company.

Uzgiris, I C and Hunt, J McV (1975). *Assessment in Infancy: Ordinal Scales of Psychological Development.* University of Illinois.

Withers, P (1991). Assessing the responses of adults with profound learning difficulties to various forms of stimulation. British Psychological Society Diploma in Clinical Psychology Dissertation, Warrington.

Wolfensberger, W (1972). *The Principle of Normalisation in Human Services.* Canadian National Institute of Mental Retardation.

Wolfensberger, W and Thomas, S (1983). *Program Analysis of Service Systems' Implementation and Normalisation Goals.* Canadian National Institute of Mental Retardation.

Woodward, M W (1959). The behaviour of idiots interpreted by Piaget's Theory of sensorimotor development, *British Journal of Education Psychology,* 29.

Woodward, M W (1979). Piaget's theory and the study of mental retardation, in Ellis, N R (ed). *Handbook of Mental Deficiency, Psychological Theory and Research,* 2nd Edition. Lawrence Erlbaum.

World Health Organisation (1980). *International Classification of Impairments, Disabilities and Handicaps: A manual of classification relating to the consequences of disease.* WHO.

Zautra, A (1983). The measurement of quality in community life: Introduction to the special edition, *Journal of Community Psychology,* 11.

Contributors

Dr Sally Cheseldine is a Chartered Clinical Psychologist, working part-time for Forth Valley Health Board and part-time on a freelance basis, carrying out staff development, training and research.

Catriona Dairon was until recently Coordinator of the Early Learning Centre, at Westerlea School. She is now Group Leader at the Scottish Centre for Children with Motor Impairments, Cumbernauld.

Jane Davidson is a Specialist Speech Therapist, working within the Speech Therapy Department of Lothian Health Board's Primary Care and Community Unit, Edinburgh.

Elizabeth Dean is a Research Fellow in the Department of Speech Therapy, Queen Margaret College, Edinburgh.

Jo Eales has been seconded from the post of Assistant Head Teacher, Westfield School, to work as National Curriculum Development Officer on the S.O.E.D. funded project (Health Education and Special Needs.)

Anne Edmonstone is Chief Speech and Language Therapist in the Mental Health Unit, Lothian Health Board.

Sue Harland is Headteacher at Oaklands School which caters for pupils with Special Needs arising from severe or profound learning difficulties.

Professor James Hogg holds the Chair in Profound Disabilities, University of Dundee, and is the Director of the White Top Centre, Dundee.

Dr Andrew Jahoda recently completed his Ph.D at Stirling University and after working in Birmingham in Community Mental Health is currently undertaking the MSc in Clinical Psychology in Edinburgh.

Christine Knight, Assistant Headteacher, Gogarburn School, is currently seconded to the post of Curriculum Development Officer (Special Needs), Lothian Region.

Maureen Lorimer is Senior Teacher and Margaret Mackay is Headteacher at Lochgelly North School, a free standing special school in Fife, presently catering for pupils with severe and profound learning difficulties.

Shona Pinkerton is a Senior Teacher at Oaklands School which caters for pupils with Special Needs arising from severe/profound learning difficulties.

Dr Philip Seed is Senior Research Fellow in the Department of Social Work, University of Dundee.

Dr Judith Watson holds the post of joint Senior Lecturer (Special Educational Needs) at Moray House College, Edinburgh

Dr Jennifer Wishart is Senior Research Fellow in the Edinburgh Centre for Research in Child Development, Department of Psychology, University of Edinburgh.

B'HAM & SOLIHULL COLLEGE OF NURSING & MIDWIFERY LIBRARY